From the

WILDERNESS

to the

MIRACULOUS

D1510760

From the

WILDERNESS

to the

MIRACULOUS

THERESE MARSZALEK

DESTINY IMAGE® PUBLISHERS, INC.

P.O. Box 310, Shippensburg, PA 17257-0310

"Speaking to the Purposes of God for This Generation and for the Generations to Come."

This book and all other Destiny Image, Revival Press, MercyPlace, Fresh Bread, Destiny Image Fiction, and Treasure House books are available at Christian bookstores and distributors worldwide.

For a U.S. bookstore nearest you, call 1-800-722-6774.

For more information on foreign distributors, call 717-532-3040.

Reach us on the Internet: www.destinyimage.com.

Trade Paper ISBN 13: 978-0-7684-3257-2
Hardcover ISBN 978-0-7684-3456-9
Large Print ISBN 978-0-7684-3457-6
Ebook ISBN 978-0-7684-9111-1

For Worldwide Distribution, Printed in the U.S.A.

1 2 3 4 5 6 7 8 9 10 11 / 13 12 11 10

Dedication

I dedicate this book to my friend, my Lord and my Savior, Jesus Christ. As You said in John 14:6, *"I am the way, the truth, and the life. No one can come to the Father except through Me"* (NLT). Thank You, Jesus, for making the ultimate sacrifice to pave the way for us to know our Father—and His love. Through Your life, death, and resurrection, You glorified our Father. May our Father glorify You through this work and may multitudes find You—and our Father's love—as we share our journey from the wilderness to the miraculous.

To Carol—
Blessings and love!
Expect a miracle!
[signature]

Acknowledgments

With heartfelt gratitude, I'd like to acknowledge and thank the many who have impacted my life and played a key role in helping me walk out God's plan so I could write about the journey.

Tom, you're God's gift to me. You have selflessly and sacrificially supported everything God has asked of me throughout the years. The way in which you've led our family with integrity and godliness will produce rich rewards in this life and the life to come. Without you and your unconditional love, the outcome of my wilderness season would have been much different and this book could have never been written.

James, Emily, and Joe, God blessed me with the great privilege of being your mom. You will impact multitudes in your generation and generations to come with the testimony you carry in your heart. I'm so proud of you and will always be your biggest fan.

Doug and Marcia, thank you for providing a wonderful haven of peace and tranquility where I've birthed several books, including this one. DoMar farm is my favorite place in the world. Many people never get to experience the great blessing of having forever friends like you. You're the best!

Janice, Rich, and Jim, you are a key part of every page of this book and of every chapter of my life. I thank God for you and am forever grateful for the countless ways you've enriched my life and inspired me to be a better person.

Honey Vanwinkle, I admire you. Instead of waiting for people to ask for help, you step up to the plate and do whatever needs to be done. Thank you for the time you've sown into helping with the Web site and other technical issues. May you reap a hundredfold blessing for every seed you've sown into my life and the lives of countless others.

Dave at the Genesis Institute, thank you for helping me navigate the wilderness and for teaching me how to invite God into the secret place of my heart. You paved the way for me to find the Father's love and allowed yourself to be used as His tool to stir the deep waters of my soul.

Ruckins McKinley, God used you to breathe life into my destiny at a critical time. You are a gift to me and to the Body of Christ. Your integrity, humility, and the accuracy through which you minister draws a plumb line so others can see clearly. Thank you for obeying God.

Cynthia Steele, Adalina Carter, and Jacqueline Johnson, you were the tools through which God brought my miraculous healing when I least expected it. I thank God for enabling me to learn more about the Father's love by observing your lives.

And to all of the DOTS in my life. You know who you are! You have been my life preservers in the wilderness. Thank you for not allowing me to quit and for demonstrating God's faithfulness in and through your life. I love you and thank God for you!

Endorsements

As relationships develop and you get to know people personally, you discover not only their strengths and weaknesses, but you begin to see God's fingerprint in their lives. This has been the case for my wife Reshma and I as we've grown to know and love Therese and Tom Marszalek and have watched the unfolding of this triumphant journey.

Therese has once again expressed the very heart of the Father through *From the Wilderness to the Miraculous* in a transparent and personal way. Her testimony will resonate deeply in all who have faced wilderness experiences, and it is a road map for those who have not yet had the privilege of a wilderness sojourn. With compassion and humor Therese leads us through her five-year journey to its conclusion—a revelation of the Father's love. At the same time she reveals the persevering faith necessary in all of its nuances to carry us from defeat to ultimate victory.

From the Wilderness to the Miraculous will pave the way for many who have never had the courage to step out of the darkness of the condemnation and shame of their past. The grace that Therese walked in during this time is in and of itself no less miraculous than the spiritual and physical healing she received. It is a great honor to recommend this riveting book to those desiring to know the love of our Father God or needing a timely word of encouragement to help them continue on their own wilderness journey. Just as Therese was encouraged through a prophetic word revealing that she would be delivered at 46, so this book encourages us that our own redemption draws near. I hear clearly in that secret place in my heart the words, "Well done, good and faithful servant." Well done, Therese!

Dr. Bruce Allen
Still Waters International Ministries
Author of *Promise of the Third Day* and
Prophetic Promise of the Seventh Day

Therese, a long-time trusted friend, allowed me to walk with her and witness her wilderness journey. Through her desert-like season, she made herself available to serve and be a friend to others in need, putting their needs above her own, even in the midst of the most challenging circumstances and crippling pain. Therese's wilderness journey and testimony of finding the Father's love have been a great source of life to me. *From the Wilderness to the Miraculous* is a personal journey that reminds us to trust in God and His promises in spite of life's forever-changing circumstances.

Julie Greenfield
Abundant Life Fellowship
Butte, Montana

Therese Marszalek's *From the Wilderness to the Miraculous* is a journey typical of multitudes hurting in the Body of

Christ worldwide. With unrestrained candidness regarding her deep woundedness, she shares her journey through emotional and physical pain, which led to her total healing. As Therese shares an ultimate revelation of a truly loving God, she leads the reader to the profound conclusion: "You are worthy by the righteous blood of the Lamb." *From the Wilderness to the Miraculous* is a well-written, easy-to-read book that will touch many lives, as Therese's other books have already done.

Dr. Flo Ellers
Global Glory Ministries

Many have been told that they are accidents of nature, void of purpose and hope. Through *From the Wilderness to the Miraculous,* Therese reminds us that even when our lives feel like a stagnant pool of pond scum, God is unfolding a wondrous destiny ahead. As you enter the pages of Therese's life, may you discover that you are not forgotten, but valued and deeply loved by the Father.

Pastor Faye Higbee
Raven Ministries

The revelation shared in *From the Wilderness to the Miraculous* was life changing! A perfect gift book for those experiencing difficult times, this anointed book will touch multitudes who are either experiencing their own personal "wilderness" or have come through the wilderness without understanding the divine purpose of their trials. While Therese guides readers through her own trials, she reminds them that God has a perfectly orchestrated plan and hasn't left us in a hostile world to fend for ourselves. Through her heartfelt words, Therese challenges readers to a greater understanding of personal trials and gently reminds each one to press forward under the Almighty's hand of love. Surely, *From the Wilderness to the Miraculous* will inspire and bring hope to every reader!

Jacqueline Johnson, MSW
Counselor

I appreciate Therese's transparency in *From the Wilderness to the Miraculous*. I was not only gripped by the intensity of her suffering and the honesty with which she wrote, but by the way in which she approached God with this same honesty. Therese's candid yet instructive journey through physical and emotional losses chart a highway for those struggling to know God's love, rest, and healing. She shows us firsthand how God can use the dry seasons of devastation and even the greatest of trials to bring understanding of our true identity and, thereby, to our divine destiny! Through the pages of this timely book, Therese answers questions like *Why can't I rest? How can I know if God really loves me? Why am I driven by the fear of failure?* Spending time with Therese in this most engaging story of her life will bring encouragement, strength, and increased faith. Therese is a real person and has a pastor's heart as she teaches us through *From the Wilderness to the Miraculous*. She is a brave soul on a great journey with our King. I love her for it.

Gena Bradford
Singer, Songwriter, and Author

From the Wilderness to the Miraculous was life changing and brought me peace, comfort, and increased faith. Therese's honesty will inspire imperfect Christians to recognize that enduring severe life trials is a normal, valuable part of life in Christ, and it is not from a lack of faith or sin. This book will encourage those walking through a wilderness season to move through it knowing that it is a season of purification where the old is passing away to bring forth God's plan that awaits.

Charity Bagatsing
Publishing Diva & Editor-in-Chief
Northwest Woman magazine

My husband and our two children were introduced to Therese Marszalek and her family through reading two of her previous books, *Extraordinary Miracles in the Lives of Ordinary People* and *Miracles Still Happen*. Although we have never met and live on different continents, our mutual love for the Lord has brought about a wonderful friendship. The subtitle of *From the Wilderness to the Miraculous* so beautifully sums up the work to which Therese has committed her life. I believe God will use *From the Wilderness to the Miraculous* to touch lives in an even more wonderful way than her previous books already have. It is beautiful to see how the Lord uses people like Therese and her husband Tom to encourage those experiencing wilderness seasons. This book demonstrates God's love for us and testifies to His faithfulness in turning our lives around from whatever despair we may be suffering to the wonderful gift Jesus offers to each of us if we will only accept it: the true peace and love that comes only from giving our hearts and lives to God.

Lorna Bradley
Drogheda, Ireland

In Therese Marszalek's book *From the Wilderness to the Miraculous,* she openly shares her triumphs but also her fears, struggles, and longing to know the Father's love. Therese ministers from understanding "what comes from the heart reaches the heart." As you read her book you'll be introduced to a wonderful wilderness buddy and will realize that you're no longer alone! You have a friend! Therese's courage and faith are contagious and will empower you to continue to walk in faith when nothing makes sense. Therese's testimony will draw you into the Father's presence and love. As you walk with Therese through her wilderness journey from beginning to end, a wonderful work of grace and hope will be birthed in your heart. Truly this book is God-breathed and timely for this season in the Body of Christ.

Becky Weber
Fragrance Ministries

"Imagine what we could accomplish for God if we not only made ourselves available to Him, but also listened and responded *only* to His direction and command." These words seemed to leap off the page as I read *From the Wilderness to the Miraculous.* Therese Marszalek is a gracious, kind woman, but she is also a warrior. A warrior who has been tried, tested, and victorious penned these words. This book brings great encouragement, and I pray it provokes the warrior in you *not* to quit, but to imagine yourself as one who is available and accomplishing much for the Kingdom of God. Therese, I love you and thank you for the privilege of reading your manuscript.

Pastor Donna Sanders
Spokane Faith Center

From the Wilderness to the Miraculous contains powerful words from a powerful woman of God. Reading about Therese Marszalek's personal journey through the wilderness is a teaching experience for all, especially those who, like me, have endured the wilderness. After recovering from cancer and surgery, and losing my wife to cancer, the Lord led me to Rosalie Willis and her ministry, A Company of Women. Not only did I marry Rosalie, but I met wonderful followers of Christ like Tom and Therese Marszalek. Although I knew Therese as a gifted writer of Christian literature and knew she had faced medical issues, I had no idea what she had experienced until I read this book. *From the Wilderness to the Miraculous* reveals the depth of Therese's devotion to God and His perfect timing. I believe everyone who reads this book will learn as they walk with Therese through her personal wilderness experience.

Robert L. "Stormy" Storment
Post Falls, Idaho

I was so excited to read Therese Marszalek's latest book, *From the Wilderness to the Miraculous*, because we are such dear friends. As I began reading, my eyes filled with tears, knowing that her and the transparency of her heart would speak with healing and amplify God's love and faithfulness to every reader. To quote Therese, "The Father's love will find you in the wilderness! He is a God of restoration and will redeem the years the enemy has stolen." This wonderful story of God's love, restoration, and healing will bring new depths of understanding to your heart.

Rosalie Willis Storment
Author and Founder of
A Company of Women International

As Christians, we walk the honest tension between being fellow strugglers and overwhelming conquerors. Therese Marszalek's *From the Wilderness to the Miraculous* serves as both a journey mate through pain and confusion, and a beacon toward refuge and hope. Therese's refreshing transparency and tested wisdom assures us that the night is, indeed, followed by the dawn. Struggle and victory, together, emboss the horizon of faith.

Judy Mandeville
Sacred dance instructor, writer, and speaker

Therese Marszalek's most recent publication, *From the Wilderness to the Miraculous,* will leave readers pondering its rich teaching long after they finish using it as a Bible study guide, devotional, or most engaging Christian "Self-Help" for pilgrims suffering from low self-worth in the wilderness. Like the Israelites, through many years of personal suffering in the wilderness, Therese learned to discern God's truth. Therese's life testifies that as we know our heavenly Father and His nature, He "deletes" satan's lies that cause us to believe that we are orphans, uncared for by the King of the Universe. Therese experienced a remarkable supernatural healing, but first had God's promise of healing, a demonstration that God's promises will come to pass since He cannot lie. Readers will be deeply reassured, gently guided, and powerfully encouraged by Therese's testimony of God's guidance in her life. I recommend it warmly!

Josiane Lynch, MA (Hons), Dip. Ed.
Brisbane, Australia

In *From the Wilderness to the Miraculous,* Therese Marszalek takes readers on a trip to *see* the heart of God, to learn to *hear* His voice, to *walk* in His pathways, and to *sit* in His presence. I loved Therese's transparency and the reality of her story! This book, a lesson in love and obedience, will enable you to see God's presence in everyday life, and reminds us that He never leaves us or forsakes us. You will indeed recognize Him as our *Father God.*

Ruth Roberts
Spokane Christian Center, minister, retired nurse,
spiritual mom, and mentor

God brought Therese Marszalek into our lives over a decade ago when my wife and I were wandering through the wilderness. Lost and hopeless, we prepared to end our marriage. When discouragement and breaking hearts led us to seek God's help, He blessed us with Therese. Through the years Therese and her husband Tom provided us counsel, comfort, spiritual guidance, and long-lasting friendship. Therese's remarkable love for Jesus has led us through the desert. It has been an incredible blessing for Marcia and I to witness Therese's journey, and in some small way to be a part of the creation of her books. I hope that through this book, your story will lead to the same conclusion of our story: There is hope and help in Jesus!

As we prepare to celebrate 18 years of marriage, we reflect and give thanks to God for His grace, love, and forgiveness, and thank Therese for helping us find the way. *From the Wilderness to the Miraculous* is Therese's best work yet. Not only is it a testimony of her faith in Jesus Christ, but also the story of a remarkable season of her life. The pages of this book demonstrate, without doubt, that God indeed works miracles in the lives of His children every day. Therese bares her soul to the reader, unashamed and unafraid to give the credit to the Father, who led her and carried her through her wilderness struggle. Enjoy the read, then give your troubles to God, stand firm in faith, and allow Him to do His work in you.

Doug and Marcia Kyser
Bethel Church of the Assemblies of God
Chehalis, Washington

Contents

Foreword by Dr. Cerullo

When I first met Therese Marszalek, she was sitting across from me on the cozy, familiar television interview set of my television program *Morris Cerullo Helpline*, which was being taped at CBS Studios in Hollywood, California. With a poised, professional demeanor, Therese animatedly described miracle after miracle after miracle from her first book, entitled *Extraordinary Miracles in the Lives of Ordinary People*. There was no doubting the validity of those miracles in the lives of countless "ordinary" people whose stories Therese had carefully documented and meticulously reported.

But, as Therese herself will quickly tell you, there is a price to pay when you serve God. Therese went through her own "wilderness" period throughout the whole time of researching, writing, editing, and publishing her first book...

And that's what her new book *From the Wilderness to the Miraculous* is all about: Therese's journey to the Father's love as she suffered attack after attack from the enemy, who was trying to stop and discredit her from giving glory to God for every miracle she wrote about.

If you are feeling discouraged today—no matter what your circumstances are—Therese's new book will encourage and strengthen your heart to press on and not give up. Your faith will soar to new heights of expectation as you read Therese's account of her own challenging journey through the wilderness—into her promised land of victory!

I heartily recommend you read Therese Marszalek's fascinating story in *From the Wilderness to the Miraculous*. Your life will never be the same!

Dr. Morris Cerullo
President and CEO,
Morris Cerullo World Evangelism

Foreword by Ruckins McKinley

From the Wilderness to the Miraculous is a moving testimony of the power of God in action. As you join Therese on her wilderness journey, you will read firsthand what it is like to trust Him at His word. The Word of God says that He watches over His word to perform it. In *From the Wilderness to the Miraculous*, you'll see one of His best performances! No matter where you are on the journey with your heavenly Father, *From the Wilderness to the Miraculous* will not only build your faith, it will heal your soul.

I highly recommend this book and pray that it touches your heart as it has touched mine.

Ruckins McKinley, DD
Generation Of Demonstration
www.generationofdemonstration.com

Introduction

God Has a Plan

God has a plan—a *good* plan—for your life! Your Creator knew you *before* you were born. He recorded every day of your life in His book and laid out every moment *before* a single day passed (see Ps. 139:16).

Your life was God's idea and your birth was no accident. Even if you were a surprise to your earthly parents, you were no surprise to your heavenly Father. He strategically orchestrated your arrival and departure according to His perfect plan. Knowing the precise number of your days on earth, He was intimately aware of every minute detail that would occur between your first and last breath.

Before you landed on planet Earth, God knew every right and wrong turn you'd make. He knew every victory, every defeat, every good decision, and every not-so-good decision to unfold throughout the course of your life. He knew the achievements you'd attain and the failures you'd experience. And knowing all that would occur throughout your lifetime—great and not so great—He had a plan, a *good* plan.

"But," you might say, "I've messed up God's plan." If you've made mistakes, or taken a detour or two, you're not alone. As you'll see in the coming pages, I made more than my share of mistakes and experienced countless miserable failures. The Bible says that *"all have sinned and fall short of the glory of God"* (Rom. 3:23). No one is immune from error—*not even one* (see Rom. 3:10).

Maybe you, like me, thought you were headed in the right direction when an unexpected detour veered you onto an unfamiliar path through the wilderness of suffering. Regardless of how you got to the point you're at today, the good news is that your failures, mistakes, or detours didn't terminate God's plan. He still has a plan—a *good* plan!

The devil wants you to think that your errors or unexpected circumstances have aborted God's ideal plan. Wanting to convince you that God has written you off, the evil one suggests that you've supposedly passed the point of no return. Stamping "hopeless" on your spiritual file, he wants you to believe that it's too late to get back on course. "Abort mission, abort mission!" he proposes.

You *are* on an earthly mission! But God, the One who sent you, will move Heaven and earth to help you fulfill it—regardless of what took place prior to this moment.

The very thought that your life's purpose could be aborted is a lie of the enemy. *"When he [the devil] lies, he speaks his native language, for he is a liar and the father of lies....There is no truth in him"* (John 8:44). God's Word, however, is truth that has been forever settled in Heaven (see John 17:17;

Ps. 119:89). The truth is that God knew every detour you'd take and every mistake you'd make—*before* you set foot on the earth.

God isn't surprised by the situation you're facing today. He's aware of your circumstances and isn't shocked by any of it. He has known about your circumstances since the beginning of time—and He's already present in your tomorrow working out the plan...a *good plan!*

Like a tailor-made suit, God personalized and equipped you for a plan that fits you—and only you—with perfect precision. He deposited natural and spiritual gifts within you, and designed, cut, and created a pattern that you—and only you—can wear. God's plan for your life, and the ways in which He equipped you to fulfill that plan, is as unique as your fingerprint.

God's purpose for our earthly sojourn unfolds through life seasons. Although most of us naturally prefer spring-like seasons of sunshine, blooming flowers, and sweet fragrances saturating the air, we'll also encounter desert-like seasons when surroundings appear bleak, barren, and dry: *The Wilderness.*

Human tendency is to resist the wilderness, but it's my hope that you'll find the courage to welcome this supernatural time, recognizing that it's a tiny slice of a much bigger picture. If you remain submitted to God and embrace this season instead of running from it, you'll discover the priceless treasures and miraculous breakthroughs the wilderness can produce. The bigger picture—a masterpiece painted on God's canvas—will be a glorious sight for all to behold!

Although we often shrink back from afflictions that abound in the wilderness, we'd benefit by acknowledging their value and realizing that God allows them for our good and for His glory. God uses trials to prune us and make us more fruitful. Although the trials of the pruning process can hurt, they test our faith, develop perseverance, mature us, and prove our faith genuine, all of which bring glory to God (see James 1:2-5; 1 Pet. 1:5-9). That's a fruitful harvest!

Trials are common in the wilderness terrain. According to Psalm 34:19, a righteous man or woman—one in right standing with God—will face trials of *many* kinds. Also referred to as troubles or afflictions, trials are a normal part of the Christian life even if you're doing everything right. Although you can't avoid trials, God will walk you *through* and deliver you *from* every single one. He promised! (See Psalm 34:19.)

Although some trials are an ordinary part of the Christian journey, others are a direct consequence of sin. Self-inflicted, sin-induced trials that often lead to wilderness seasons differ greatly from those orchestrated by God. With God's help, we can discern the difference!

God laid out His perfect will in His flawless written Word—including boundaries and disciplines—for our good. Obeying His revealed will leads us on the path to an abundant life. Rebelling against His will eventually lead to consequences, which often manifest themselves as trials.

The nation of Israel's rebellion led them into numerous trials where they faced stiff consequences. Words similar to those introducing the story of Gideon—*"Again the Israelites did evil in the eyes of the Lord"* (Judg. 6:1)—are repeated throughout Old Testament Scriptures.

Israel opened the door to the enemy by disobeying God's command to follow no god but the one true God. They paid a penalty for their sin when, for seven long years, God gave them into the hands of the Midianites. This fierce enemy invaded Israel's land, destroyed their crops, and chased them into the mountains. Although sin and poor choices had invited this trouble, when Israel called out to God for help, He heard their cries and sent Gideon as a deliverer.

We're not much different from Israel when it comes to sin and poor choices. God clearly laid out His expectations through His Word and told us which path leads to abundant life. Yet at times we ignore God's direction, opening the door for stiff consequences and creating opportunities for the enemy to ravage us as he ravaged Israel.

Although we can blame the devil for our self-inflicted treks through the desert (for which he is happy to take credit), we would benefit by humbling ourselves before God, acknowledging the error of our ways, and repenting. Like Israel, when we sin and repent God hears our petitions for help and responds with a special deliverer even greater than Gideon: Jesus!

Whether we're suffering as a consequence of sin, or if we're being crushed under the heavy hand of Midianite-like bondage, Jesus is *"an ever-present help in trouble"* (Ps. 46:1).

Jesus, who had no sin, delivers us from sin and makes us righteous before God (see 2 Cor. 5:21). If we'll admit the error of our ways and repent, God is faithful and just to forgive our sin and promises to cleanse us of all unrighteousness (see 1 John 1:9). We've been given a great privilege through the shed blood of Christ to wipe the slate clean and start anew.

Do you need help? Call out to God with genuine transparency. Repent, call on the name of Jesus, and let Him lift your load. Do it now, before we head into a God-ordained wilderness where our Beloved awaits us.

Remember Psalm 139:16—God knew every day and every moment of your life before you set foot on earth. He knows what you're walking through today. He's aware of your marital issues. He knows the circumstances you're facing with your children; He sees your workplace stress. He knows your financial state. He knows every detail of your relationships. He knows your body's physical condition. He knows what's happening in your church. He knows every detail—without exception—of everything in your life. And He has a plan—a *good* plan!

Before We Begin...

You're about to walk through my wilderness experience, not as a spectator, but as a participant. On this exciting personal journey, you'll not only reap the treasures I discovered along the way, but you'll uncover glorious riches of your own.

But first things first. Before you join me in the wilderness, I encourage you to locate the "I Am Here" point on your life's map. You need to know where you are right now before you can determine where you're going!

My husband Tom, who favors the latest and greatest technology, discovered a device that benefits directionally challenged people like me who have difficulty navigating the highways and byways. Tom installed a global positioning satellite (GPS) receiver in one of our vehicles, a gadget he fondly refers to as Penelope.

Penelope is an amazing device. When we program a destination address into Penelope, she senses the exact starting position via satellite, then provides step-by-step directions until we reach our final destination. "In 500 feet, turn left," Penelope advises. "At the next intersection, go straight." Whether on a cross-country trip or a quick jaunt into town, Penelope knows the way.

If we take a wrong turn or miss an exit, it's no problem for Penelope, the wise GPS! "Make a U-turn at the next available road," she says, then continues with directions from the current position to steer you back on track. Penelope, unlike humans, doesn't get frustrated with other drivers and never makes jokes about directionally challenged people like me. I like her!

Once while visiting family in the Midwest, we headed to my brother Rich's home for dinner. Penelope led us into St. Paul, then directed us to turn off the freeway at a specific exit. Certain that Penelope was in error, I suggested that Tom ignore her directions and instead go another way—*my way*. After all, I had lived in the Twin Cities for 30 years before moving westward! Of *course* I knew how to get to my brother's home.

Penelope was right. I was wrong. We arrived late, thanks to my stubborn refusal to follow Penelope's instructions. "Your destination is on the left," she said, without mentioning my error.

God's Positioning System (GPS), a supernatural guidance system, is available to direct you on the road of life and is an absolute necessity for wilderness journeys.

When you acknowledge your "I Am Here" point and surrender your life to Jesus, God's Positioning System senses your current position, then directs you toward your divine destination. Regardless of where you begin—or how many wrong turns you've made in the past—God offers a tailor-made travel plan.

Unlike Penelope, He knows all travelers intimately, loves them unconditionally, and offers them comfort along the bumpy roads. Unlike Penelope, God's GPS doesn't need programming as He is pre-programmed with personal routes ideal for all who invite Him on their journey.

The Bible, God's instruction manual, is also a must for your earthly travels. Even when you try your best to follow His instructions, however, you may encounter some unexpected detours or even lose your way. If you veer off course or miss a turn, fear not! God will meet you at your current location, direct you to the next available U-turn, then point you in the right direction.

If you've been directionally challenged and have gotten off course or wandered unexpectedly into uncharted territory, God's Positioning System can steer you back on track and will lead you on the route He knows is best for you. Allow God to program His flawless destination plan into your heart, then purpose to follow His instructions.

Highways and byways crisscross road maps like a complex vascular system, providing endless options for would-be travelers. Although plotting the ideal course for a cross-country trip can be accomplished with a good road map, maps don't exist for wilderness journeys.

Although we may think we see the best route, our near-sightedness often blinds us from much that lies ahead. God, however, sees the big picture, knowing the beginning, the end, and everything in between. If you stick close to Him, you'll avoid bunny trails that lead nowhere.

Your journey through the wilderness may require more time or effort than you expected or thought you could tolerate. God, unlike us, isn't concerned about time. To Him, a day is like a thousand years and a thousand years is like a day! He's more interested in the fruitful growth being produced in us as we navigate through the wilderness terrain. He cares about the *process*.

Israel, God's chosen people, became familiar with the wilderness. In Egypt, they had suffered greatly under the heavy hand of a ruthless Pharaoh (see Exod. 3). Buckling under the pressure of slave masters who oppressed them with harsh forced labor, Israel cried out to God.

Concerned when He saw the misery and heard the desperate cries of His people, God sent Moses as a deliverer. *"The cry of the Israelites has reached Me,"* He told Moses, *"and I have seen the way the Egyptians are oppressing them. So now, go. I am sending you to Pharaoh to bring My people the Israelites out of Egypt"* (Exod. 3:9-10). God always makes help available and keeps His promise to deliver us from every trial—in His time.

Through a wondrous string of supernatural miracles, God delivered Israel from 430 years of bondage in Egypt and set them on a path destined for the land promised to their forefathers, a land flowing with milk and honey. Yet their unbelief and rebellion resulted in a detour. A journey normally requiring 11 days (see Deut. 1:2) turned into a 40-year trek through the desert!

After Israel's escape from Egypt, God could have led them on the road passing through Philistine country—the shorter route. But knowing that if they faced war, they might change their minds and return to Egypt, He instead led them via the desert road toward the Red Sea (see Exod. 13:17-18).

God didn't abandon Israel during their extended wilderness journey, but faithfully escorted them every step of the way. By day He went ahead of them in a pillar of cloud and by night He guided them in a pillar of fire. God cared for their every need—in 40 years their clothes didn't wear out! (See Deuteronomy 8:2-5.)

As Israel journeyed, God tested them to expose what was in their heart, and to see whether or not they would keep His commands (see Deut. 8:2). God already knew what was in their hearts as He knows the heart of every person, but *they* needed to see what was in their hearts—and *they* needed to choose their response.

The condition of their hearts—not the distance—stood between Israel and their promised land. The Great Physician had to perform spiritual heart surgery and teach them key lessons necessary for survival in the land that flowed with milk and honey. Fierce enemies awaited them in the land of promise; they had to learn how to fight! Without God's training, Israel surely would have perished.

God allowed Israel to experience pain and suffering, both necessary for their preparation and training. Through desert training, Israel saw God's greatness and realized their fallen sinful condition, prone to rebellion and doubt. And the bloodline, through which Jesus, the Savior of the world, would come—had to be preserved. God had a plan for every minute detail.

God, in His great wisdom, didn't simply transport His chosen people from point A (Egypt) to point B (the Promised Land), He prepared them to live in obedience to Him once they arrived at their destination.

Your spiritual pilgrimage through the wilderness may be lengthy, painful, and discouraging at times just as it was for Israel—and for me. Be encouraged! God will not merely enable you to survive this wilderness season; He will prepare you to live a surrendered life of service and devotion to Him as you enter the Promised Land of His abundant life!

God rarely works things out as we think is best or most convenient and seldom takes us on the shortest path to our destination. Instead, He leads us on the course *He* knows is best, *even if it takes 40 years to get there!*

Have you acknowledged your "I am here" point? Your Egypt may not be a pretty picture at the moment, but with God in the driver's seat, He will make all things beautiful—in His time. From your vantage point, it may appear as if insurmountable obstacles are sure to hinder your ability to move forward, but your Guide will take you around or over those roadblocks—in His time.

If you've surrendered yourself—and your wilderness season—to the all-knowing God, His spiritual satellite has located you and will enable you to reach your final destination right on schedule.

Learn from Israel! Complaining or resisting the path God has chosen for you will only extend your wilderness season and make you miserable. Instead, choose to relax and cooperate. God has a plan—a *good* plan!

Chapter 1

A Glimpse Into the Wilderness

Meditation

Seasons of wilderness, where trials and troubles are plentiful, are a normal aspect of Christian life. My Father knows every detail of the trial I'm facing right now. He knew it was coming, He knows my current circumstances, and He has a plan for my deliverance—a *good* plan!

Scripture Focus

A righteous man may have many troubles, but the Lord delivers him from them all (Psalm 34:19).

What is my Father saying to me through this Scripture?

May my meditation be pleasing to Him, as I rejoice in the Lord (Psalm 104:34).

My Dream

In the dream, I sat amongst a sea of people listening to a speaker who appeared to have been clothed in God's glory. Radiating unspeakable joy, she patted her heart and with tender emotion declared, "My Father *loves* me!" Smiling heavenward with outstretched arms, she again beamed, "He *loves* me!"

Bewildered, I stared at her in stunned silence. *My Father loves me* echoed in my heart like a resounding gong. *What does that mean?* I wondered. *What would it feel like to know that my Father loved me?* It seemed as if she was speaking a foreign language for which I needed a translator.

A sudden desperation arose from the depth of my soul. I *had* to know the love this woman had discovered. I *had* to find this love of which she spoke.

Leaning forward in my seat, I peered closer in disbelief. The speaker was *me!*

The truth had been revealed: I didn't know God's love, yet I longed for it from afar. The dream, a Heaven-sent glimpse of the Father's desire for me—and you—to delight in knowing His love from center stage, launched me into a wondrous journey that would transform His ultimate desire into a living reality.

But the journey on which I would soon embark would be a difficult one.

At a ministry luncheon on March 5, 2003, Fran Lance, the guest speaker, ministered prophetically. Speaking to me she said:

> The Lord says He's bringing you face to face in combat with the enemy, but He has trained your arms for war. You're a mighty warrior and you've got ammunition in your hands to destroy the works of the

enemy. I sense that's the writer in you. Through the writings that God is going to produce in you, you're going to defeat the enemy on every side. He gives me Psalm 145:6, *"They will tell of the power of Your awesome works, and I will proclaim Your great deeds."* Lord, we thank You that she is a proclaimer of who You are.

I had never crossed paths with Fran Lance before—or since—that day, yet the prophetic word spoken through her left a fingerprint on my heart. I tucked the tape-recorded message away, a bit bewildered at receiving advance notice that God was about to bring me face to face with enemy combat.

Like a spiritual oxymoron, skirmishes with evil enemy forces expressed in the prophetic word soon paralleled the discovery of God's love as demonstrated in my dream. Both would come to pass during a five-year wilderness season of intense suffering, which I will share in the coming pages. But God had a plan. He *always* has a plan!

Would a loving God lead His children into the wilderness where they may face combat with the enemy of our soul?

Jesus, God's only begotten Son, is no stranger to confrontations with satan and is certainly no stranger to the wilderness. After Jesus' baptism in the River Jordan, the heavens opened as the Holy Spirit descended on Him in the form of a dove. His heavenly Father said, *"This is My Son, whom I love;*

with Him I am well pleased" (Matt. 3:17). A perfect picture of tranquility!

Yet immediately after receiving this fatherly kiss from above, Jesus was *led by the Spirit* into the wilderness where He spent 40 days and nights being tempted of the devil (see Luke 4:1-13). "Tempted," the Greek word *peirazo*, means "to test." In the wilderness, Jesus underwent an intense time of testing.

It doesn't seem to make sense. God the Father had just affirmed and expressed His love for His Son—a sinless man. Fully God yet fully human, Jesus was in perfect standing with His Father—yet led *by the Spirit of God* into a season of testing? Would a loving Father lead His only begotten Son to a place of suffering?

Human reason might tempt us to cry, "No fair!" "Foul!" "Unjust!" Yet God, in His great wisdom, had a plan. He *always* has a plan!

A wondrous miracle of transformation and empowerment developed in the wilderness. The Bible says that *"Jesus, full of the Holy Spirit...was led by the Spirit"* into the wilderness to conquer every temptation (test) that confronted Him (Luke 4:1). After enduring a 40-day testing period, He emerged from the desert transformed *"in the power of the Spirit"* (Luke 4:14). As news about Jesus spread throughout the countryside, God launched Him into His earthly ministry, which led to Calvary where He would fulfill His Father's plan to save the world from sin.

God may send you, as He did Jesus—and me—into a wilderness season of testing where you'll encounter trials of many kinds. But even in the parched desert lands of affliction, God is faithful and has a plan! A *good* plan.

If God sends you into the wilderness where trials are as plentiful as the grains of sand in the desert, it isn't to punish you or because you've done something wrong. Although satan's shaming and blaming lies can sound quite convincing, the truth is that God may be doing a supernatural work in you that He can accomplish *only* in the wilderness. Even when you're doing everything right, you may find yourself—often with no advance notice—on a wilderness journey where you will encounter intense suffering. I did. I'm a wilderness survivor—and you can be too!

If you're a recent wilderness arrival or if you're battle-weary after camping out in the desert long-term, don't give up! Don't quit! God is up to something good and He's not done with you yet. Let Him accomplish what He needs to accomplish in you.

For the joy set before Him, Jesus endured the cross (see Heb. 12:2). Because Jesus saw you—the joy set before Him—He endured the wilderness. For the joy set before you—those who need the fruit that God is developing in you—you can endure the wilderness too.

Embrace Jesus in the wilderness. He's been there and knows what you're facing. He won't let you be tempted (tested) beyond what you can bear, and will provide a way out so you can endure (see 1 Cor. 10:13). Like Jesus, as you remain submitted to God, you *will* emerge from the desert transformed—*in the power of the Holy Spirit*—and a testimony in your mouth!

Near the end of his life, Winston Churchill returned to Harrow, his old school, to address students preparing to launch into new life adventures. Although his message lasted less than a minute, it was never forgotten. "Young men," he said, "don't give up. Never give up. Never, never, never, never give up."

God will walk you *through* the wilderness and will take you from testing and trial to triumph. Don't give up. Never give up. Never, never, never, never give up! Your Promised Land is ahead!

For Reflection and Discussion

1. Think back to the dream shared at the beginning of this chapter. Ask yourself: do I relate more to the speaker who expresses confident delight in knowing the Father's love or to the one in the audience, who longs for, yet does not know, the Father's love?

2. Reflect on and describe your current or most recent wilderness experience.

3. Luke 4:1-13 says that Jesus was *"led by the Spirit"* into the wilderness where He spent 40 days and nights being tempted by the devil. Relate this to your beliefs regarding seasons of testing in your life.

4. What have been my most prominent attitudes during wilderness seasons? Have I embraced the experience as an opportunity to grow? Have I blamed my Father for the suffering I had to endure? Have I wondered if the Lord is punishing me for past failures or mistakes?

Reflect on what I am saying, for the Lord will give you insight into all this (2 Timothy 2:7).

Prayer of Repentance

Father, forgive me for the times I've questioned Your faithfulness or blamed You for my suffering. Cleanse me of any sin or flawed beliefs that have hindered my ability to see the value of the trials I experience and help me replace any lies I've believed, with the Truth of Your Word.

Other areas of repentance:

Repent, then, and turn to God, so that your sins may be wiped out, that times of refreshing may come from the Lord (Acts 3:19).

Prayer of Submission

Father God, as I continue my wilderness journey, I surrender wholly to You—body, soul, and spirit. Open my eyes that I might see clearly; open my ears that I might hear Your voice; open my mind that I might learn Your lessons; and open my heart that I might become more like You. Have Your way in me, Lord. I believe You will complete the good work You started in me, and I trust that You know the best way in which to accomplish that good work. In Jesus' name.

Other areas of submission:

Submit yourselves, then, to God (James 4:7).

My Personal Words From My Father

_____

_____

_____

From the Father's Heart

My child, I extend My hand of love to you. Come, take My hand as I lead you from the valley of trial to the mountain of triumph. My righteousness shall go before you in the wilderness, and My glory will be your rear guard. Whatever you face, you will never be alone as I will never leave you or forsake you, and will walk with you all the days of your life.

Speak, Lord, for Your servant is listening (1 Samuel 3:9).

Chapter 2

Famine in the Land

Meditation

The Creator of the universe, my heavenly Father, loves me!

Scripture Focus

How great is the love the Father has lavished on us, that we should be called children of God! And that is what we are! The reason the world does not know us is that it did not know Him (1 John 3:1).

What is my Father saying to me through this Scripture?

May my meditation be pleasing to Him, as I rejoice in the Lord (Psalm 104:34).

"How Did I Get Here?"

"How did I get here?" Did you ask that question when you unexpectedly found yourself in the desert of trial? I did. If God had allowed me to cast a vote for or against my wilderness journey, I surely would have voted against it, hands down! Yet having come through the wilderness, I thank God for His wisdom in not granting me a vote.

Although unpleasant, painful, and abounding in uncertainty, my wilderness walk led me to the fulfillment of my greatest desire: a revelation of the Father's love. After discovering His love, which changed me forever, I wouldn't trade my wilderness for all the jewels in the world!

One might assume that a Christian who had walked with God for more than two and a half decades, and had preached and written about God's love, would possess a well-developed revelation of that love. I would assume the same, especially considering that God, the Creator of love, *is* love (see 1 John 4:8). After all, His love is the foundational truth of Christianity.

Some aspects of love seemed simple to me. I understood that Jesus loved me, realizing He had given His life to pay the penalty for my sin. I knew that the Holy Spirit, my Helper and Counselor, loved me too. Understanding God's command to love others was no problem either.

Knowing the love of Father God, however, was anything but simple. I knew God loved everybody else. After all, John 3:16, *"For God so loved the world that He gave His only begotten Son, that whoever believes in Him should not perish but have everlasting life"* (NKJV), was the first verse I had ever memorized. Believing that God the Father loved me personally, however, seemed impossible to grasp. The Father's love seemed incomprehensible, unreachable.

Scriptures about God's love seemed to apply to everyone but me. Although I could recite the love Scriptures, it was merely mental assent. My hidden belief system, of which even I was not consciously aware, whispered, "You're an exception. Those Scriptures apply to everyone else...except you." "Rejected," "shameful," and "unworthy" shouted through the megaphone of my warped identity.

If someone said, "God loves you," I nodded my head in agreement while crossing my spiritual fingers behind my back. I yearned for God's love, yet my lack of worth left me unable to receive even the crumbs that might fall from His table. Instead of feasting on the abundant love He made available, I was love starved.

Our surface beliefs often differ from what lies in the deep, hidden waters of our soul. Hidden belief systems that contradict God's Word stem from the devil's lies. Because those lies breed great distress and hinder us from enjoying the fullness of life that God promises, thank God when those lies are revealed!

As a child, I starved for my earthly father's love too. Dad, a diligent worker and man of strong character and integrity, struggled with severe clinical depression that made him emotionally unavailable to me.

Although Dad didn't talk about his faith, he brought us to church on Sunday mornings—without fail. During the Catholic mass, I often stared at the cross hanging in the sanctuary. Seeing the crown of thorns, and His spiked hands and feet, I imagined the trauma Jesus must have endured. I didn't understand why Jesus—a good man who had healed and helped people—had to suffer so greatly.

Week after week the same questions played through my mind: *Who did that to Jesus? Who crucified Him?* I felt overwhelmingly drawn to Jesus, whose suffering troubled me deeply. Jesus' crucifixion bothered me for many years to come, yet my questions remained unexpressed and unanswered.

Dad's battle with depression made expressing love difficult for him. Physical affection of any kind was non-existent. He worked long hours to provide for our family and at home found solace behind the newspaper. I longed for his love and attention but didn't know how to compete with the newspaper.

Hearing my friends communicate and laugh with their dads seemed odd to me. Witnessing other dads hugging and kissing their kids seemed even stranger. Yet I secretly envied what they had.

Children need to know that Daddy loves them and approves of them; they need Daddy's hugs and kisses, and need to know Daddy is proud of them. Kids need to know Daddy will protect them from danger and harm. They need to know that Daddy loves them unconditionally.

Across our land, a famine of the father's love has left countless people, men and women alike, love starved. Multitudes have been raised fatherless for one reason or another, some even when the father is physically present but absent in every other way.

Resident in every person is a God-given desire for love. Sadly, children lacking their earthly father's expression of love often find it difficult to receive their heavenly Father's love. Although God freely gives love to His cherished children, warped belief systems like mine make some unable to freely embrace it.

Without an understanding of God's love, people often pursue avenues that fall far short of God's ideal plan. While searching for love in all the wrong places, some develop addictions, and others seek promiscuous relationships. Some, like me, develop a performance drive, and others choose dangerous paths leading to further self-destruction and intense pain.

Misguided years of seeking love outside of God's design have set the stage for and led to wilderness experiences for multitudes around the world. But there's good news! The Father's love will find you in the wilderness! He is a God of restoration and will redeem the years the enemy has stolen.

As a child longing for Dad's love, I strived, unconsciously trying to earn his approval through my accomplishments. I worked diligently in school to bring home straight A's and excelled in endless activities to gain Dad's affection. But affirmation and affection never came.

I learned to set my expectations low at an early age, as disappointments didn't hurt as much that way. Eventually when my emotions deadened, disappointments didn't hurt at all. Detached from my feelings, I eventually became unaware of my lack. I didn't feel good; I didn't feel bad. I didn't feel at all. As far as I was concerned, I was fine. Below the surface, however, I wasn't fine at all.

I continued to strive. The more I worked, the more I accomplished, and the more I accomplished, the more I excelled, and the more I excelled the greater measure of worth I felt.

The day I turned 15, I applied for my first job, and by 17 I had earned enough to pay cash for a new car. Fueled by a performance drive and need for approval, by day I attended high school and by night I managed a restaurant.

My fruitless endeavors to gain Dad's attention led me to believe a lie that, for some reason, I was unlovable. When disappointments reminded me that I wasn't loved, I unconsciously stored the experiences in a secret chamber of my heart marked, "Keep Out." When making disappointment deposits, I always shut the door to that secret place quickly before any tears could slip out. I never entered that chamber and didn't allow anyone else to enter. Not even God.

In the workplace I was a valued employee as my drive enabled me to accomplish the work of several people. I completed my duties with excellence and fulfilled my overcommitted plate of activity without fail. People knew they could count on me, a highly responsible young adult.

No matter how much I accomplished though, I couldn't shake the feeling of being "less than enough," "not good enough," and "not worthy enough." Although my lack of self-worth didn't show on the outside, it simmered inside, driving me to push until I could push no more. Although I had done more as a young adult than some do in a lifetime, to me it wasn't enough. It *never* would have been enough.

In spite of my inner turmoil, the appearance of happiness and success followed me. Outwardly my life painted a picture of independence, a prosperous career, a fat bank account, and popularity amongst my peers. Friends and co-workers didn't realize, however, that the pillar of strength they saw on the outside was crumbling on the inside.

Smiling through a love-starved heart, I deceived those around me. My outer contentment masked the torment imploding. The false illusion fizzled as a cloud of anguish surfaced. I felt restless. And my questions about Jesus' unjust suffering, which had gripped my heart from childhood, were still on my mind.

Increasing awareness of an inner emptiness demanded attention. Trying to fill the cavernous hole, I searched for love through a string of unhealthy promiscuous relationships and partying. Driven into compromising situations and dysfunctional relationships, I often misinterpreted men's attention for the love I craved. Desperate for love and affection, I didn't realize—or care—that I was being used and abused.

Unable to fill my emptiness, I cried out to the God I wasn't certain even existed.

God heard the cry of my heart and sent my brother Jim with a book containing the answers I had searched for all my life.

I read T.L. Osborne's *How to Be Born Again* from cover to cover. Each Scripture-laced page further unfolded the truth that I was lost in sin and needed a Savior. God lifted the spiritual veil and opened my blind eyes. I needed Jesus, the only One who could fill the emptiness I had been trying to fill.

The cross I had stared at as a child flooded my memory; the unrest I had sensed seeing Jesus on the cross saturated my soul. I found the answer to the question that had haunted me throughout my life: *My sin* put Jesus on the cross. I had crucified Jesus. I sent Him to the cross of Calvary where He suffered the punishment I deserved—and He did it willingly for me.

After repenting of my sin and accepting the sacrifice He made for me, I invited Jesus into my heart. Although I felt unworthy, He accepted my broken life. Dropping to my knees, I surrendered. "My life belongs to You, God," I prayed. "Make me the person You want me to be."

I would soon learn that God took my words seriously.

For Reflection and Discussion

1. Describe your relationship with your earthly father.

2. Describe your relationship with your heavenly Father. How has your relationship with your earthly father impacted your relationship with your heavenly Father?

3. In what ways have you tried to earn your earthly father's love and approval? In what ways have you tried to earn your heavenly Father's love and approval?

4. Say out loud, "I am worthy of my Father's love." How does that statement make you feel? Tell Father God what you feel about your sense of worth. Ask Him how He feels about your worth to Him. Write down what your heavenly Father whispers into your heart.

Reflect on what I am saying, for the Lord will give you insight into all this (2 Timothy 2:7).

Prayer of Repentance

Father God, forgive me for the ways I have resisted and doubted Your love for me. I'm sorry, Father, for striving to earn Your love and approval, instead of receiving them as the gifts You willingly and freely offer me.

Other areas of repentance:

Repent, then, and turn to God, so that your sins may be wiped out, that times of refreshing may come from the Lord (Acts 3:19).

Prayer of Submission

Loving Father, I want to come to You with childlike faith, but I don't know how. As I crawl into Your lap, teach me what I need to learn from You. Help me erase beliefs that painted the wrong picture of You or that don't align with Your Word. Help me, Father, to rewrite our love story. In Jesus' name.

Other areas of submission:

Submit yourselves, then, to God (James 4:7).

My Personal Words From My Father

_____

_____

_____

Speak, Lord, for Your servant is listening (1 Samuel 3:9).

From the Father's Heart

I welcome you, My child, with arms open wide. How I have longed for you to draw close to My heart. How I have longed for you to embrace and walk in the fullness of My love. As we navigate the wilderness terrain together, I shall blot out everything that does not testify of My love and will expand your understanding of Me. As you know Me with increasing measure, you shall know My love with increasing measure, for *I Am* love.

Chapter 3

Broken Pieces

Meditation

God has a plan for my life! A *good* plan!

Scripture Focus

"For I know the plans I have for you," declares the Lord, "plans to prosper you and not to harm you, plans to give you hope and a future" (Jeremiah 29:11).

What is my Father saying to me through this Scripture?

May my meditation be pleasing to Him, as I rejoice in the Lord (Psalm 104:34).

Hungry for God

Hungry for God, I attended the only church I had known to feed my spiritual starvation, yet I left unfed, unfilled, and unsatisfied. The familiar repetitious prayers and traditions made church lifeless. And I didn't know enough to seek spiritual guidance.

My decision to follow Jesus quickly faded. If poor choices cornered me in a crisis situation however, I cried out to Him, offering spiritual bargains in exchange for His rescue. My God-seeking was self-centered and temporary. I never followed through with my end of the bargain. I'd walk away from Him to pursue worldly lusts. But He never walked away from me.

I entered a stormy marriage where fear, deception, and emotional abuse became a daily staple. My well-established lack of worth enabled me to tolerate being mistreated and disrespected, feeling as if I deserved it. Although I maintained a good career, I wore shame like an invisible blanket.

In the fall of 1987, while I juggled a demanding career and a crumbling marriage, my firstborn son, James, arrived. Six weeks later, his father announced that he no longer wanted to be married. He had planned ahead, rented an apartment, and opened separate financial accounts.

Memories flashed as my worst fears manifested. Months before James' birth, my husband had frequented the bars after work hours, leaving me at the dinner table with only my growing belly. Seeing the empty place setting, I wondered why he didn't include me in his social life. I became accustomed to being left out, ashamed that the only place my husband seemed to have any use for me was in the bedroom. Even there, I felt used, then discarded. Yet I feared losing him. I didn't want to be alone, even if it meant being miserable. I didn't know that God had a better plan.

After my husband announced that he was leaving our newborn son and me, I begged him not to go, desperate to hang on to the very life that was destroying me. But he had made up his mind.

He walked out, seemingly unmoved by the mountainous despair he left behind. Like a double-edged sword, the abrupt death of the marriage thrust deep wounds in my heart that would soon scar over before healing was complete. But God knew about my wounds, and had a perfect plan to heal me.

Alone and frightened, hopelessness enveloped me and further reinforced my belief that I was unlovable. Outwardly though, the independent, confident person I projected continued to deceive others. Wiping my tears away, I pushed the rejection and abandonment aside, and poured myself into my career. For James's sake, I pressed on.

After trying to shoulder my pain alone for several months, the load became more than I could bear. Consumed with grief, I came to the foot of the cross in prayer, but this time I didn't offer God bargains in exchange for my rescue. Surrendering my life—again—I laid my failed marriage and shattered life at Jesus' feet. Emerging from behind my invisible mask, I offered Him all I had: mistakes, failures, and broken heart.

Remembering the decision I had made years earlier to follow Christ, my heart flooded with God's love. I remembered the cross. I remembered Jesus and I remembered the blood He shed for me. And I felt clean—again.

As if taking me by the hand, Jesus poured His grace and mercy into my fragile emotions, gathered the broken pieces of my life, and began to rearrange them for a new future. Day by day, His grace lifted me higher as He walked me from the valley of anguish into a season of renewal. Hope in Jesus fueled me to focus on building a new life for James and me.

Like a prodigal daughter, I ran into the Father's open arms who had patiently and lovingly waited for my return. Vowing to never leave Him again, I purposed to know the One who gave His life for me. And for the first time, I opened a Bible and read it cover to cover.

My well-established performance drive followed me into my renewed relationship with God. Still wearing an invisible cloak of unworthiness, I unconsciously believed that if I could *do* enough for God, I might earn His love and approval. I had much to learn.

While I healed from my failed marriage, God sent a remarkable man into my life who helped me learn to love and trust again. Tom's uncompromising integrity and tenderness of heart refreshed my soul. I admired his strength, compassion, and unconditional love. Tom was protective of me, something I had never experienced before. And it felt good.

Tom courted me, treating me like a queen, respecting me as a woman, and honoring me as a mother. Because I had been accustomed to abuse, his love was unfamiliar, even uncomfortable. Although my discomfort caused me to push Tom away at times, he patiently taught me how to receive genuine love.

James and I moved to Seattle in late 1990 to start our new life with Tom. Entering into Christian marriage, we made God the core of our covenant relationship. Determined that every aspect of our lives would revolve around God and His Word, we believed God would see us through anything we might face.

Soon after we were married, Tom adopted James, committed to love and provide for him as his own.

On Christmas Eve, only days before our first anniversary, our beautiful daughter Emily Carol arrived. Although I had an established career, Tom and I discussed the importance of raising our children. I struggled with the possibility of leaving my job as my identity was still wrapped up in my performance. In my mind, stay-at-home moms watched soap operas and ate bon bons, neither of which appealed to me whatsoever!

As I contemplated the upcoming change, a wise friend's words clinched the decision. "You can always reestablish a career," she said, "but you'll never be able to raise your kids again." Leaving my 12-year career at Honeywell, I committed to full-time motherhood—and never looked back.

On Valentine's Day two years later, Joseph Thomas, another delightful bundle of joy arrived, making our family complete.

Our growing family stayed the course as God continued to teach us His ways. As a young mother, I established a spiritual diet to feed my spirit and nourish my soul, delving into God's Word daily. Little did I know that the words being written on the tablet of my heart would sustain me during the wilderness journey right around the bend.

In the fall of 1998, shortly after we relocated from Seattle to Spokane, Washington, God unexpectedly prompted me to write a book, an endeavor I had never desired or considered. During a praise and worship service, He downloaded the title, 12 chapter titles, and a vision of the cover artwork into my heart.

He must have the wrong person, I thought. I had never written anything for publication. Reminding God of my many shortcomings, I said, "But Lord, I have no talent...no time...no experience...no...."

"What *do* you have?" He seemed to ask.

All I had to offer was a desire and willingness to obey Him. And for God, that was enough.

In between child-rearing activities, I pressed through each step of the publishing process in countless revisions and rewrites. While submitting magazine articles to build my writing resumé, I accumulated enough rejection letters to paper my office walls. But doors began to open wide. As I persevered and remained committed to the process, God blessed my writing and provided opportunities for me in multi-denominational publications throughout the country.

With my book close to completion, I registered for a writer's conference, anticipating the next step to finishing the project with which God had entrusted me. The zeal I arrived with deflated as I listened to a staff evaluation of a chapter from my manuscript. "People have heard these same things before," she criticized in a condescending tone. "There's really nothing new here."

Feeling as if I had been kicked in my spiritual womb, a wave of nausea hit me. I thanked her, excused myself, and discretely headed to my car. As soon as I shut the car door, tears flowed. I *thought* God had told me to write this book. I *thought* I had obeyed God. I had invested thousands of hours of writing and prayer into this project that I *thought* had been ordained by God.

I returned to the conference, but my mind was elsewhere. *I must have imagined that God told me to write this book,* I thought. *What was I thinking?*

When the conference ended, I made a beeline for the door. I cried all the way home, then tossed and turned all night, certain I had disappointed—and unknowingly misrepresented—God. Sick to my stomach, I felt as if I had committed the unpardonable sin. Although Tom tried to comfort and reaffirm me, I was inconsolable.

The next day, my puffy bloodshot eyes in the mirror reminded me of my supposed failure and tempted me to skip Sunday morning service. "God, please forgive me," I prayed. "I didn't mean to misrepresent You." "Lord," I vowed, "I'm shelving this book. I'll *never* write again." And I meant it.

We arrived at church where Prophet Ruckins McKinley, a guest minister whom we had never met, was scheduled to speak. After preaching, he motioned for Tom and me to come to the platform. With closed eyes, he spoke by the Spirit of God:

> I see God taking out that in which you have said "never mind" and bringing it back to you far greater than you realize. For the Lord says, "Woman of God, your eyes tell many stories, yet your stories must be heard. Through your writings will I touch many." For the Lord says, "Don't shelf it. Don't let it go. For there is a creative ability inside of you. I even see children's books on the inside of you and other things that you have yet to write and publish." And God says, "This is the hour in which I will take out of the darkness and bring a great light and out of that light will come healing and hope for many others and many families because of that in which I am doing through you for the 21st century."

God wasn't going to let me quit and wouldn't allow someone's misguided words abort His plan for my life.

Refueled with a heavenly reminder of God's call to write and publish, I continued writing and persevered until I completed the book. The process of submitting proposals brought more rejection letters, which I later learned was normal in the publishing industry. Eventually, I secured a publisher.

Less than two and a half years after the Lord had directed me to write that first book, I held a copy of *Breaking Out*, a replica of the vision God had initially shown me. I had published over 100 magazine articles, secured a second publishing contract with the finest Christian publisher, completed a third book, and had developed and taught writer's workshops and seminars to equip others with the tools and encouragement needed to launch into writing.

What I thought was impossible, God made possible, doing immeasurably more than I had asked or imagined. All He needed was a willing heart.

For Reflection and Discussion

1. Gather and describe the most prominent areas of your life when you believed you had failed or made a significant mistake. How have you viewed those experiences? With blame? Shame? Guilt? How do you believe your Father views your mistakes and failures?

2. Describe experiences that discouraged or tried to derail God's plan for your life.

3. Recall the people or circumstances God has used to encourage you in times of discouragement. Thank Him!

4. Has God asked something of you that you believe will be impossible to accomplish? Explain why it seems impossible. Make note of what you *do* have to accomplish, what your Father asked of you, even if you have only a desire to obey Him.

Reflect on what I am saying, for the Lord will give you insight into all this (2 Timothy 2:7).

Prayer of Repentance

I admit, Father, how often I've tried to hide my brokenness from You. I acknowledge how often I've tried to fix my mistakes and failures without inviting You to be the center of my restoration. I'm sorry, Father. Forgive me. Although I've shared only certain areas of my life with You in the past, I desire to bring every aspect of my life to You now. Here I am, Lord. I give myself to You.

Other areas of repentance:

Repent, then, and turn to God, so that your sins may be wiped out, that times of refreshing may come from the Lord (Acts 3:19).

Prayer of Submission

Father, I've gathered the broken pieces of my life and release them into Your loving hands. I give You my shame, my mistakes, my pain, and my broken heart. I give You everything that led me to this very moment with You. I surrender my will to Your will and ask that You rearrange my broken life into Your masterpiece where my plans and desires are Your plan and desire. In Jesus' name.

Other areas of submission:

Submit yourselves, then, to God (James 4:7).

My Personal Words From My Father

_____

_____

_____

Speak, Lord, for Your servant is listening (1 Samuel 3:9).

From the Father's Heart

My Child, I rejoice in receiving what you perceive as your broken pieces. As you trust Me with your life, I surely will create a masterpiece for all to behold. And through the once broken places, My glory shall shine and bring great light to others to set captives free. I'm making all things beautiful in My time and will turn your broken pieces into precious treasures that even you shall value more than priceless jewels.

Chapter 4

Time Out

Meditation

It is equally important to obey my Father when He directs me to take a "time out" for rest and refreshing as it is to obey His direction to "go" and "do." Has my Father asked me to take a "time out?" Have I obeyed Father God's promptings to rest?

Scripture Focus

Then Jesus said, "Let's go off by ourselves to a quiet place and rest awhile" (Mark 6:31 NLT).

What is my Father speaking to me through this Scripture?

May my meditation be pleasing to Him, as I rejoice in the Lord (Psalm 104:34).

Another Book

God stirred my heart to write another book as He turned my attention to the war, crime, deterioration of the family, and breakdown of society's morals that filled the pages of the newspaper and dominated television news. Yet in the midst of the hopeless reports, I saw God doing wondrous miracles around the globe—which were rarely reported. The absence of God's miracles in the media troubled me.

As I prayed, the Lord illuminated Psalm 145:6. *"They will tell of the power of Your awesome works, and I will proclaim Your great deeds"* leapt off the pages of the Bible and branded my heart. Receiving His Words as a personal mandate to share God's wondrous works with the world, I welcomed the open door to proclaim His great deeds. A co-author and I set out to document miracles God was doing in the earth, rejoicing at the opportunity to give God some press!

As I collected and wrote miracle testimonies, my performance drive fueled a constant flurry of demanding pursuits. While juggling my overflowing plate of responsibilities, I fretted regularly. If nobody stepped up to the plate when needs arose, I jumped in without consulting God. I was never at rest. I had no time to rest.

I continued working on the miracles book while earning a master's degree from Bible college, working on a third book, freelance writing for magazines, volunteering at schools and church, and trying to fulfill my role as wife, mother, and friend. While I rescued needy projects and people who crossed my path, my marriage and family rattled out of balance.

Physically and spiritually exhausted by age 40, I felt God whisper in my heart, *I'm putting you in a time out.*

The time had arrived. God was about to send me into the wilderness, a season I had unknowingly been preparing for throughout my life. I entered the wilderness at age 40, the prophetic number meaning *wilderness*.

"Why would I need a time out, Lord?" I asked.

"You need to learn to trust Me and rest in Me," He seemed to whisper.

What? I thought, puffing up with pride. *I've served Him for over 20 years: I have a master's degree from Bible school...I've preached and written countless articles about trusting God...of course I know how to trust and rest in Him. Aren't trusting and resting in Him covered in Christianity 101?!*

Examining my heart and eventually humbling myself before the Lord, I faced a stark reality: I had no clue how to trust or rest in God. I didn't even know what the words meant! Trust and rest were as foreign to me as was the concept of God's love.

"I don't know how to trust You, Lord," I admitted. "And I don't know how to rest." Surrendering to Him, I entered God's time out: *The Wilderness.*

After over 40 years of excellent health, migraine headaches started arriving several times a week. When increasing fatigue plagued me daily, I pressed through it and forced my body to cooperate. I refused to rest, unwilling to bow down to defeat.

Although I didn't understand why sickness had touched my life, I knew that God didn't author it. Sickness and disease are *not* from God, nor does He inflict sickness on people to teach them lessons. Jesus came to heal the sick and those oppressed of the devil (see Acts 10:38). He forgives all of our sins and heals all of our diseases (see Ps. 103:2-3). He was pierced for our transgressions and crushed for our iniquities. The punishment that brought us peace was upon Him, and by His wounds we are *healed* (see Isa. 53:4-5). God would *not* contradict His Word by sending sickness or disease. What a silly thought!

Sickness and disease, however, are part of our fallen, sinful world, and if we face infirmities, God won't waste the opportunity to teach us as we walk *through* them and will use what the devil intended for evil for our good and for God's glory.

Barely able to function, I suffered from chronic fatigue from the moment I woke until retiring for the night. When my doctor ordered a sleep study, I hoped it would reveal my core problem. After electrodes were connected to my brain, limbs, chest, and fingers, the lights went out. "Lord," I prayed, "grant me a good sleep. *Please* show them what's wrong with me."

Unable to fall asleep, I tossed and turned all night and as a result, the medical staff was unable to evaluate or diagnose my sleep disorder.

Gripping my steering wheel on the drive home from the hospital early the next morning, I felt tears dripping into my lap. My patience had been depleted. "God, I asked a simple thing of You. I only wanted to sleep so they could evaluate me."

Pounding my fist on the steering wheel, I pleaded. "Why? Why couldn't You have given me such a simple thing? Why!?"

My hopes dashed for diagnosing and treating my fatigue, I landed back at square one. Although I felt I hadn't made any progress, God was at work, making progress according to His perfect plan. Heaven's lessons, assigned in God's perfect timing, provided opportunities for me to learn how to trust God when nothing made sense.

How I wished for an easier and quicker answer. Most, like me, would likely prefer a less challenging path to the spiritual growth and maturity needed in God's Land of Promise.

Shortcuts. Human nature seems equipped with a built-in radar that scans the terrain for a shorter, easier path to our destination—regardless of what that destination happens to be.

An advertisement for a supposed weight loss shortcut once grabbed my attention: *New Skinny Pill*. Featuring a slim, perfect-figured beauty, the manufacturer promised, "Lose up to 15 pounds a week with the amazing formula that forces your body to release fat! As much as 4 inches and 50% of all excess fat gone in just 14 days!" Anyone willing to send in his or her cash could "eat, miss no meals, and enjoy all sorts of food, morning, noon, and night." Advertisers boasted of the supernatural pill's ability to provide a miraculous shortcut to slimness. "Melt away fat 3 times faster than jogging 4 miles a day, 12 times faster than a full hour of military aerobics."

Wow. Imagine losing unwanted fat with only the mere effort it takes to swallow a pill! Eat, drink, and be merry as the pounds melt away? No sacrifice? What a deal!

Through the medical concoction in this pill to paradise, short-term weight loss may be possible; however, long-term health is highly unlikely. Maintaining a healthy, slim body requires much more effort and sacrifice than popping a pill. Instead, it requires eating a healthy, balanced diet, getting adequate exercise, and knowing when to say "no" to second helpings. Long-term health calls for a lifetime of diligence and effort. Shortcuts to weight loss hold no weight!

Spiritual fitness needed to endure the wilderness doesn't develop by popping an amazing "spiritual pill" either, though many would likely take advantage of such a pill if it were available—especially if it meant avoiding the wilderness trek where God's personalized training program awaits them.

Imagine an advertisement for a supernatural spiritual pill: Gain a lifetime of spiritual knowledge, wisdom, and Christian experience in only two weeks with the amazing formula that forces you to release holiness. As much as 50 percent of all excess sin gone in just 14 days! You can live however you want and enjoy whatever you want, morning, noon, and night. Become spiritually mature 3 times faster than studying Scripture for 40 years or leading Bible study for 10 years, and 12 times faster than a full hour of daily prayer!

Although laughable, we often prefer shortcuts to spiritual maturity and are unwilling to make the effort or sacrifice necessary to grow. People don't develop godly wisdom and gain spiritual revelation because they label themselves Christian or because they attend church on Sunday mornings. The journey in Christ, maturing and growing in faith, doesn't magically appear by following a magic formula.

Christian maturity develops over time—a lifetime. Spiritual growth requires meditating on God's Word and renewing our mind to His ways. It means a commitment to spending time in the throne room of prayer, nurturing our relationship with God, and living a life of obedience to His Word. It requires a willingness to sacrifice for the good of others and serving even when it inconveniences us. And it often includes a journey or two through the wilderness.

Spiritual maturity costs something. An abundant life of ongoing Christian growth requires a surrender of all: body, soul, spirit, and will to God. Full surrender to the lordship of Jesus will mold and transform one into the image of Christ, a supernatural metamorphosis that no miracle pill could ever accomplish.

For Reflection and Discussion

1. Have you experienced a "time out"? Describe what led to that time out and what you learned during that "time out." Are you in a "time out" or do you need a "time out?" Explain.

2. Identify destructive patterns in your life that seem to repeat themselves. Ask your Father for steps you can take to overcome these destructive patterns. Document those steps and keep them before you daily.

When you are ready to submit to and commit to your Father's direction, with whom can you share this information for accountability?

3. What does *trust* mean to you? Describe what *rest* means to you. Reflecting on your relationship with your Father in Heaven, what level of trust and rest do you have currently and what would you like to see change?

4. Count the cost of submitting to and committing to the *process* through which your Father wants to take you so you can grow. Be quiet and listen to the still small voice of the Holy Spirit. When ready, verbalize your commitment to your Father.

Reflect on what I am saying, for the Lord will give you insight into all this (2 Timothy 2:7).

Prayer of Repentance

Father of compassion, I've been so overburdened and over-committed, and have ignored and disobeyed Your promptings to come away for a time of rest and refreshing with You. Forgive me, Father God, for filling my life with clutter and leaving little time for You. My priorities, O Lord, are out of balance. Have mercy on me, O God. Wipe my slate clean, through the cleansing blood of Your Son, Jesus, that I might start anew.

Other areas of repentance:

Repent, then, and turn to God, so that your sins may be wiped out, that times of refreshing may come from the Lord (Acts 3:19).

Prayer of Submission

Loving Father, I give You my plans, schedule, and daily agenda. Help me discover and implement the proper balance spiritually, emotionally, and physically. Help me prune my schedule and make me willing to let go of that which isn't part of Your divine plan. Help me, Lord, to identify areas needing change and enable me to submit to those people You put in my life to help bring that change. Help me, O Lord, to make Your priorities my priorities. In Jesus' name.

Other areas of submission:

Submit yourselves, then, to God (James 4:7).

My Personal Words From My Father

_____

_____

_____

Speak, Lord, for Your servant is listening (1 Samuel 3:9).

From the Father's Heart

My precious child, I shall lead you and guide you by My Spirit and will help you find the balance you need to flourish and grow. Seek Me *daily*, and surrender your plan to My plan *daily*. I have prepared you in advance for the works I planned for you to do. Do not fret about your schedule, My child, give it to Me. I will put wondrous surprises in your path as you keep your eyes focused on Me. As you are about My business, I AM about your business.

Chapter 5

Dilemma of Depression

Meditation

My Father always knows what I'm feeling emotionally, physically, and spiritually. Wherever I go, my Father knows where I am. My loving Father, the God of all comfort, will meet me and love me, right where I am.

Scripture Focus

Where can I go from Your Spirit? Where can I flee from Your presence? If I go up to the heavens, You are there; if I make my bed in the depths, You are there. If I rise on the wings of the dawn, if I settle on the far side of the sea, even there Your hand will guide me, Your right hand will hold me fast (Psalm 139:7-10).

What is my Father speaking to me through this Scripture?

May my meditation be pleasing to Him, as I rejoice in the Lord (Psalm 104:34).

Physical Struggles

Migraines and incapacitating fatigue continued to afflict me. No longer able to force my body to cooperate, I slept often during the day yet never felt refreshed. My sense of worth having always been dependent on my accomplishments, I despised lying down because doing nothing left me guilt-ridden. But while I wasn't doing anything, God *was* doing something.

My friend Gena, another driven woman whom God was home schooling about resting in Him, suggested that I join her for prayer ministry on July 22, 2003. A rather private person, I wasn't accustomed to sharing my personal needs with others and felt uncomfortable asking for help. Yet desperate for relief, I agreed.

Gena and I met with Connie Hice and Cyndi Cederblom at the Assemblies of God Church in Medical Lake, Washington. My pulsating temples and screaming joints and muscles must have been evident as they encouraged me to lie on the floor while they prayed.

For over four hours the loving prayer warrior trio soaked me in prayer, willing to continue longer if necessary.

Speaking by the Spirit of God, Connie said,

God is taking you on a journey. The Body of Christ needs to know what you learn on this journey. He is going to teach you about the Father's love, intimacy with the Father. At times it will be very painful, at times you'll feel scared, and at times you'll feel like you're losing your mind.

Gena documented the prophetic word spoken through Connie Hice. Those God-breathed words, tucked away in a Bible and forgotten for several years as they came to pass, would not emerge again until I later emerged from the wilderness.

Hearing *God is going to teach you the Father's love* stirred the deep waters of my soul. I hungered for His love, was spiritually dissatisfied, and knew God had more for me than what I had experienced. I had studied His Word with diligence, prayed and tried to draw close to God, yet it seemed as if a Plexiglas barrier separated me from His fullness. I could see what I longed for; I could feel it. I could almost taste it. But I didn't know how to break through the spiritual barrier to find the wondrous God for whom I hungered.

Continuing deeper into foreign territory, I found myself slumped in my office chair one afternoon. Hoping to write, I pulled out a book of matches, then lit the tea light nestled inside a beautifully crafted angel. I stared at the flame dancing on its uplifted golden trumpet. The angel sat on my desk as a reminder of God's call to proclaim His Word. Posted next to my laptop was, *"They will tell of the power of Your awesome works, and I will proclaim Your great deeds"* (Ps. 145:6).

But I didn't want to proclaim anything. Feeling lost, defeated, and alone, I blew out the candle, shut down my computer, and stared at the blank screen. Depression had gripped me. Not only was I in pain, I was scared. And I felt as if I was losing my mind.

I didn't understand what was happening to me. In years gone by, people had marveled at my exuberant energy. I proudly accepted my title "Superwoman," knowing that without God's strength fueling me, I was like an ink pen with a dried-up inkwell.

Strange emotions of defeat settled like a black cloud. Uncertainty and loneliness bewildered me. Although I'd experienced the temporary sadness that everyone feels occasionally, this was different. With physical and emotional energy depleted, my ability to function normally was impaired beyond my control.

Brain fog made simple decision-making a major endeavor. Still battling chronic fatigue, my drive to fulfill the tasks on my to-do list dissipated. I wondered if I was tired because I was depressed or depressed because I was tired.

When my family asked what was wrong, I couldn't answer. I canceled appointments so I could be alone and avoided answering the phone. When I had to be around people, I expended great energy trying to appear normal. Feeling like a phony, I wished I could flee to isolation.

I didn't get it. In spite of my recent physical health challenges, I had been blessed with a good life and enjoyed serving in various ministries. I had a loving husband, a fruitful marriage, and three awesome children. It didn't make sense for me to feel depressed.

A tormenting thought replayed like a broken record: *I can't be depressed...I'm a Christian.*

I had heard many well-intentioned messages thunder from the pulpit claiming that depressed people simply needed more faith...they ought to pray more...seek the joy of the Lord...reach out to others instead of focusing on themselves. Preachers said depressed people just needed to "get over it." At the time, I agreed with a hearty "Amen!" Yet now, their words echoing in my mind cloaked me in shame.

I cried in private, unable to express my feelings to God or to anyone. The Prozac jokes I once laughed at, weren't funny anymore. And I dreaded the thought that someone might discover my secret.

I examined my heart to see if a seed of unforgiveness might have taken root to sprout the misery. I searched my conscience to see if other sin had opened the door for despair. But I found no explanation for the downward spiral I was experiencing.

After the dark cloud lingered for several weeks, I became desperate. Fighting the thought that I had failed God, I tried to pray, but could only muster the strength to cry, "Help me, God!"

God answered my cry for help by leading me to resources and people to help me better understand and overcome depression.

I called Dad, who had suffered from depression throughout his adult life and had been hospitalized numerous times during my childhood. Dad's depression, a taboo subject, had never been discussed in our home.

Dad wept as I described my symptoms. I learned that my grandfather and several other close relatives also had suffered from depression. Dad advised me to seek medical attention. "Don't feel ashamed," he encouraged.

How can I not feel ashamed? I thought. *I've failed as a Christian.*

I feared that exposing my depression would squelch my Christian influence. As an author and inspirational speaker, I had written and preached about God's provision for health—body, soul, and spirit. I wondered if people would consider me a spiritual failure if they knew I was unable to live God's abundant life of which I taught. I was *supposed* to have the joy of the Lord; I was *supposed* to walk by faith; I was *supposed* to be an overcomer; I was *supposed* to be strong. The negative stigma of depression haunted me.

Swallowing my pride, I scheduled a doctor's appointment. After evaluating me, she explained the various causes for depression, one being an imbalance of certain brain chemicals called neurotransmitters. She said depression was a common medical condition requiring treatment.

The doctor prescribed a temporary mild anti-depressant to balance serotonin levels. It wouldn't cause any major change, she said, but would gradually and subtly bring brain chemicals into harmony. When I hesitated, she asked, "Would you refuse medication or treatment if you were diagnosed with liver disease or cancer?"

"Of course not," I answered. But this seemed different. Liver disease and cancer were justifiable illnesses. Depression, I thought, was unacceptable.

Taking the written prescription, I slinked out of her office. On the way home, I sped past the pharmacy without a glance, trying to resist the overwhelming self-condemnation.

Eventually I mustered the courage to fill the prescription. Facing the neighborhood pharmacist magnified my embarrassment. I swore my husband to secrecy and shared my depression secret with no one.

As the doctor predicted, I didn't notice a drastic change after taking the medication for several months. I felt increasingly better, however, and didn't suffer episodes of lingering black clouds.

When able, I confided in two trusted friends who committed to pray for me. Exposing my struggle lifted a heavy burden. One friend, who also had fought depression, recommended a timely book that answered many questions. Another friend suggested that I play praise and worship music in my home, another key that brought comfort during my recovery.

Because severe fatigue continued to plague me, doctors ordered additional medical tests. Blood tests confirmed Hashimoto's Thyroiditis, an autoimmune disorder in which the body's immune system mistakenly attacks the thyroid gland. Because the thyroid is like the central control system of the body, if it malfunctions, other physical systems can malfunction also. After seeing more specialists and under-going additional tests, I was diagnosed with fibromyalgia. Depression is a common symptom of both of these auto-immune disorders.

In time, God revealed the causes of my depression and led me to a successful treatment plan. Unwelcome and unexpected cycles of depression would revisit from time to time, but when I sensed the black clouds moving in, I had a support system to call on for help. And the storms passed much easier.

The angel on my desk would continue to remind me of God's directive to proclaim His great deeds. Free from the shame and bondage of depression, I could move forward to fulfill God's plan with a better understanding and greater compassion for other depression sufferers.

Depression, when a person experiences deep, unshakable sadness and diminished interest in normal activities, affects an estimated 17-18 million Americans every year, making it one of the most common medical problems in the United States.[1] Depression is also common—and often misunderstood—in the wilderness. Whether it's been part of your wilderness season or not, gaining a better understanding of the dilemma of depression will enable you to benefit others who might be struggling with this fragile physical, emotional, and spiritual challenge.

Depression is a medical condition, not a character flaw or weakness. Yet, because of the negative stigma attached to it, many suffering from depression avoid seeking treatment.

Some are embarrassed or fear others will view it as a sign of personal weakness.

Although most people experience a temporary sadness, loneliness, or blues occasionally, depression can impair a person's ability to function normally[2]. Feelings of guilt, despair, hopelessness, worthlessness, and even thoughts of suicide are common. Symptoms of depression can include difficulty concentrating or making decisions, memory loss, changes in eating and sleeping habits, loss of interest in normal activities, and difficulty working or fulfilling daily responsibilities. Episodes can be brief or long lasting, and symptoms can be mild to severe.

Prayer, desperate prayer that couldn't be formed into words, was a key that opened the door to heavenly intervention on my depression battlefield. Because the process started through prayer is often an ongoing one, those suffering with depression must patiently endure the process through which God brings them. His answer to our plea may come in the form of doctors, medication, counseling, books, or compassionate people who willingly walk with us through the valley. Thank God for creating these resources and avenues to wholeness!

Because the root cause of depression is unique to the individual, the journey to overcoming depression is also unique. In the process of submitting to and implementing God's tailor-made plan for recovery, hold your head high—or encourage someone else to hold their head high—knowing you're taking steps toward a healthier life.

For Reflection and Discussion

1. Have you experienced depression or do you know someone who has suffered from depression? Describe the experience and explain what you learned from it.

2. What has been your attitude toward people suffering from depression? Do you ever judge those experiencing physical or spiritual issues with which you are unfamiliar? Have you felt judged or misunderstood while suffering from a physical or spiritual condition? Explain.

3. What actions might you put in place to help yourself through times of discouragement or physical suffering? Do you have a trusted prayer partner that you can call? If not, ask your Father to lead you to the right person.

4. When you face emotional, spiritual, or physical challenges, do you run to your Father for help? If not, to whom do you run? Tell your Father how you feel when you come to Him with your needs.

Reflect on what I am saying, for the Lord will give you insight into all this (2 Timothy 2:7).

Prayer of Repentance

Father, God of my Lord Jesus Christ, I cry out for mercy and grace, for I have sinned against You. Forgive me for judging myself and others for areas of suffering I did not understand. I've been prideful, trying to find answers on my own, and often unwilling to accept the answer You send my way. Take my shame, Lord; remove my guilt, Father. Make me a person of understanding, and grant me a double portion of Your compassion, that I might comfort others and myself with Your unconditional love.

Other areas of repentance:

Repent, then, and turn to God, so that your sins may be wiped out, that times of refreshing may come from the Lord (Acts 3:19).

Prayer of Submission

Father, I bring You my burdens and lay them at Your feet. I'm casting it all upon You for I know that You care for me. You are my first source of strength and counsel, O Lord. As I seek You, I believe You will bring trusted relationships into my life, who will enable me to grow closer to You and who will allow me to be transparent without worry of judgment or disapproval. And Father, use me to encourage and comfort others who are experiencing difficult circumstances. Here I am. Make me Your hands, Your feet, and Your voice. In Jesus' name.

Other areas of submission:

Submit yourselves, then, to God (James 4:7).

My Personal Words From My Father

_____

_____

_____

Speak, Lord, for Your servant is listening (1 Samuel 3:9).

From the Father's Heart

When you are lonely, come to Me. When you are afraid, trust in Me. I receive every burden, big and small. I welcome all cares, expressed and unspoken. How I long for you to give Me your burdens daily, that you could walk in freedom. As you release your cares to Me, I give you My yoke. Take up My yoke, for My yoke is easy and My burden is light. Come, My child, talk freely to Me about what is on your heart. Don't hold anything back. Your cares, big or small, are My cares, for I care for you. Pour out your heart to Me, as King David poured out his heart.

Endnotes

1. *Johns Hopkins Medical Handbook* (New York: Rebus, Inc., 1995); Phyllis A. Balch, CNC and James F. Balch, MC, *Prescription for Nutritional Healing, Third Edition* (Medletter Associates Inc., 2000).

2. *Johns Hopkins Medical Handbook*, p. 456.

Chapter 6

Word in Season

Meditation

My Father knows every wound in my heart, even those which are still hidden from me. He will heal my wounds in His perfect time and in His perfect way.

Scripture Focus

"Can anyone hide from Me in a secret place? Am I not everywhere in all the heavens and earth?" says the Lord (Jeremiah 23:24 NLT).

What is my Father speaking to me through this Scripture?

Four More Years

In September 2003, a year into the wilderness, Reverend Flo Ellers of Global Glory Ministries invited me to participate in a miracles conference in Mount Lake Terrace, Washington. Flo asked me to talk about *Miracles Still Happen,* the book I had co-authored, which had just been released. Although I wasn't feeling well, I accepted the invitation and made the six-hour drive to Western Washington.

During the conference, Mary Jenkins, Smith Wigglesworth's spiritual daughter who was in her mid-90s at the time, ministered prophetically while seated at the front of the church. Although a woman of few words, wisdom and spiritual revelation flowed freely when she opened her mouth.

"How old are you?" she asked.

"Forty-two," I said.

"Your breakthrough is coming at forty-six!" she said, pointing her finger at me with confidence. "Forty-six!" she declared again.

This was not good news! I was 42—46 was four years away! Sinking back into my seat I thought, *Four* **more** *years?*

Little did I know that the suffering I had already experienced was only the beginning birth pains of a arduous journey through physical suffering and combat with the enemy—but a glorious journey that would lead to a great reward: knowing the Father's love.

Growing medical concerns paralyzed my life. In addition to being diagnosed with Hashimoto's disease and fibromyalgia, which caused chronic pain from the top of my head to the soles of my feet, a second sleep study revealed a sleep disorder that caused 35 awakenings per hour. When I was able to sleep, turning over caused tender joint pain to awaken me once again. Lack of quality sleep left me in a brain fog throughout the day, which I often referred to as "fibro fog."

A neurological disorder caused my hands and head to shake uncontrollably and made my limbs jerk throughout the night. My joints and muscles ached around the clock. Severe weakness, numbness, and tingling in my hands and arms made normal activities difficult, often impossible. As health trials invaded more aspects of my life, I became increasingly aware of how much I had taken my good health for granted in the past.

Continuing through a medical maze, I visited a long string of specialists who provided a variety of diagnoses. Reports of possible MS, Parkinson's disease, sleep apnea, and other diagnoses were suggested, all leading to a bunny trail of tests, medications, and various courses of medical treatment. But all led back to square one. Over 163 prescriptions were tried, few of which brought relief to the symptoms. Many medications created new symptoms that mimicked other diseases, further complicating an already complex case and adding to the mountainous medical costs.

Mounting health problems brought almost all writing projects to a screeching halt. Although I was tempted to decline my column in the *Inland NW Christian News*, a publication I had written for since 2000, I sensed the Lord whisper in my heart, "No. Let *Me* close that door in *My* time."

I'm thankful that God stopped me from laying the column down prematurely as it became like a lifeline in the desert of suffering. Although I had little strength and felt mentally foggy, writing my column challenged me spiritually and provided an avenue to process my wilderness experience on paper.

Trying to appear strong in front of others required great effort, but I made the effort as I didn't want to create unnecessary concern for family or friends. Most had no idea what I was enduring as my physical appearance was quite normal. Although I had been accustomed to hiding emotional suffering, I found it more difficult to hide physical suffering. I could silence emotions, but couldn't muffle the boisterous voice of physical pain.

Feeling locked in a cocoon of suffering I saw no way of escape. But, like the butterfly's great struggle in the cocoon is necessary to strengthen its wings so it can fly once it breaks out of the cocoon, my struggle was necessary. God was strengthening me, preparing me to fly!

But the struggle within wasn't over; God still had much work to do in me. With much of my attention concentrated on my medical needs, buried emotional wounds of the past seemed to be forgotten. But God remembered. And He set His plan in motion to bring those wounds to the surface where He could heal them.

Administering inner healing through avenues that I didn't anticipate or desire, God allowed painful emotions to emerge from the depths of my soul. Yet that inner healing could not take place until I confronted stuffed emotions that had been simmering deep in my heart.

When our church family encountered unexpected turmoil, I grieved deep in my spirit, not realizing that the circumstances taking place in the church had touched a long forgotten trauma from my past. Never had I experienced such intense anguish of soul. For weeks, tear-soaked tissues multiplied throughout the house. My reaction to the church circumstances wasn't what I considered normal, yet I couldn't seem to shake the grief.

My dear friend Gena called unexpectedly. "I just finished a book that I thought you might enjoy," she said. "The next time you're out and about, stop by and pick it up, OK?"

The next day, I swung by Gena's house not realizing I was unknowingly walking into a divinely orchestrated set up.

After we greeted each other in her front yard, Gena asked, "How are things going at your church?" Her out-of-the-blue question invited more tears to well up in my already puffy eyes. Choked up, I couldn't answer.

"Can you come inside so Jack and I can pray for you?" she asked.

I nodded, still unable to talk.

Inside, Gena and her husband, Jack, began to pray. I hung my head, then tears turned on like a leaky faucet.

While they prayed, I saw a vivid vision of a sword in my heart.

"Therese," Gena said, "the Lord is showing me a sword in your heart."

Still sobbing, I nodded, shocked at the instant confirmation of the vision I had seen.

"Has there been adultery in your church?" she asked.

"Yes," I wailed.

"Has there been deception?"

"Yes," I cried, squeezing my eyes shut tighter almost as if I could make it all go away.

"The Lord is showing me that the pain you're feeling is related to your previous marriage," Gena said. "The emotional and spiritual pain of adultery and deception were thrust into your heart like a sword long ago, and it wounded you deeply. But instead of allowing yourself to feel that pain, you disconnected from it and ignored its presence. Now, you've been suffering the anguish from the adultery and deception that occurred in the church—as if you had experienced it personally."

Flashing back I remembered my ex-husband leaving me after James's birth. I remembered the adultery. I remembered the deception. And I remembered the abandonment. Although I had silenced and ignored the pain at the time, I had carried it like a sword thrust in my heart ever since. Now, the smoldering agony had surfaced in what felt like emotional torture.

"The Lord wants to take the sword from your heart, Therese. He wants to heal you today," Gena said. "Will you allow Him to take the sword from your heart?"

"Yes," I said.

As this loving couple continued to pray, my burden lifted, then evaporated. The torture over, the grief gone, I felt brand-new. The sun shining outside complemented the joy beaming in my heart. I smiled, realizing that God had set me up to set me free.

Driving home, I remembered how deeply concerned Tom had been about my emotional unsettledness since the church turbulence had occurred. Although anxious to tell him about the breakthrough, I wondered how I could possibly explain the unique ministry time I had just experienced at Gena and Jack's home.

As I described my experience, God opened Tom's spiritual eyes. "That makes total sense!" he said with a big grin. Not only had God lifted my burden and healed my wounds of the past, He lifted Tom's burden for me.

"You even look different, Hun," he said. "Your joy is back!"

In awe of God's goodness, I felt a twinge of God's love shoot through my heart like a Valentine's Day arrow. And I welcomed it.

For Reflection and Discussion

1. Describe what you feel about the length of your wilderness season. Have you experienced frustration or disappointment at how long your Father is taking to deliver you? Explain.

2. Have you had to let go of anything you considered precious during the season through which you're walking? Have you lost anything that you believed was important? What is your attitude about that which you've had to give up?

3. When people try to help you, have you accepted their help? Do you try to make it on your own or are you

willing to embrace those whom God brings into your life to help you? Have you walked in humility or pride? Explain.

4. Through what avenues has your Father sent encouragement to you in the wilderness?

Reflect on what I am saying, for the Lord will give you insight into all this (2 Timothy 2:7).

May my meditation be pleasing to Him, as I rejoice in the Lord (Psalm 104:34).

Prayer of Repentance

Gracious Father, I don't even know what hidden wounds I have buried in my heart. I'm sorry, Lord, as throughout my life, I have stored away my pain without even realizing it. Who am I to think that I know better than You? Who am I to determine what I most need? Although I haven't always processed my life experiences in the right way, I want to learn now. Help me, Father, as I can't do anything without You.

Other areas of repentance:

Repent, then, and turn to God, so that your sins may be wiped out, that times of refreshing may come from the Lord (Acts 3:19).

Prayer of Submission

Loving Father God, light of my life, I surrender my heart to You once again. I invite You to bring the hidden areas of my heart out into the open where I can see. Give me ears to hear the words of those You bring into my life for healing, and make me sensitive to the Holy Spirit that I might respond to Your leading. Have Your way in me, Father. I submit myself to You and trust You to heal wounds of the past that I might be able to glorify You in a greater measure. I am Yours. In Jesus' name.

Other areas of submission:

Submit yourselves, then, to God (James 4:7).

My Personal Words From My Father

_____

_____

_____

Speak, Lord, for Your servant is listening (1 Samuel 3:9).

From the Father's Heart

I delight in you, My child. Those hidden areas in your heart have never been hidden from Me, for I was there since the beginning. My plan for your healing, body, soul, and spirit, is a glorious plan, a divine plan, a plan that was birthed out of My unfailing love. You have not missed My timing. We are right on schedule. Today is the day of salvation. Put your head on My shoulder and let Me hold you on the journey to wholeness. For I am your healer.

Chapter 7

Growing Pains

Meditation

When my Father challenges me, He also provides the strength and everything I need to get the job done.

Scripture Focus

For I can do everything through Christ, who gives me strength (Philippians 4:13 NLT).

What is my Father speaking to me through this Scripture?

May my meditation be pleasing to Him, as I rejoice in the Lord (Psalm 104:34).

A God of Miracles

Near the end of 2004, body-wide pain made every day a unique challenge. Walking had become increasingly difficult; my hips felt as if they might break in two. Climbing stairs, I pulled myself from step to step using the banister. At night, recurring dreams of living in a wheelchair tormented me. Upon waking, my arms were like dead weight. After wiggling fingers, then wrist, then arm, feeling was eventually restored. Once I "woke up" one arm, I'd use it to shake the other one awake. Some days the numbness returned and other days a prickly tingling sensation traveled between my shoulders and fingertips.

With minimal strength, even opening the peanut butter jar became impossible. Styling my hair turned into a major task that often required too much effort to even attempt. *Sacrifice of praise* took on a richer meaning at church when I could raise my hands in praise to the Lord for only a few seconds before I simply couldn't hold them any longer.

In the midst of this tumultuous time, God directed me to write my next book, *Extraordinary Miracles in the Lives of Ordinary People.* The mountainous project seemed impossible considering that simple daily tasks had become more than I could accomplish. Yet, when I had surrendered my life to God, I committed to obey whatever He asked of me. And I meant it.

"Yes, Lord," I said. "I'll do it!" My spirit embraced the project wholly. My body, however, would take time to cooperate.

As I sat before the Lord with blank paper, it seemed as if He lifted the fogginess and replaced it with crisp clarity. With a keen sense that I was on holy ground, I began to write while God downloaded five specific directions for the book.

First, *He had chosen 50 miracles for this book. Not 49. Not 51. Exactly 50.* Remembering that 50 was the number of jubilee and the number of Pentecost—when the promised Holy Spirit was poured out upon the waiting Church—I anticipated a mighty outpouring of the Holy Spirit.

Second, *He would orchestrate and divinely connect me with those He had chosen to share their story.* And He did. One weekend I made the six-hour drive from Spokane to Seattle to visit a special elderly woman we knew as Grandma Ruth. That weekend, Art and Olita Pope were filling in for the regular facility managers at the elderly residence home where Grandma Ruth lived. During our visit, Grandma invited Art into her apartment and asked him to share his miraculous story about receiving a new knee.

Listening to Art's testimony, I knew it was one of the 50 miracles God had chosen for the book. I jotted down Art and Olita's phone number and we agreed to arrange an interview at a later date.

Over the next months I tried—unsuccessfully—to contact Art and Olita. I dialed the number Art had given me, called information, tried their employer, and even searched the Internet. When *Extraordinary Miracles in the Lives of Ordinary People* was nearly complete, I petitioned God. "Lord," I prayed, "I believe Art's story is supposed to be in this book, but I can't find him! If You want Art's story included, You'll have to bring him to me."

A few days later, my phone rang. "Is Therese Marszalek there?" the familiar voice asked.

"I was just praying for you!" I told Art, recognizing his distinguishable accent.

"We've never been to Spokane," Art explained, "but through some very odd circumstances, plans changed and... here we are! When we arrived unexpectedly in Spokane, your ministry card fell out of Olita's purse and she said, 'Look, Art! Therese Marszalek lives in Spokane. Let's call her!'"

God brought Art and Olita to me, just as I had asked! Although their stay in Spokane was brief, we met several times to document their miracle story. Like Art and Olita Pope's story, every miracle included in *Extraordinary Miracles in the Lives of Ordinary People* had been supernaturally performed by God and supernaturally chosen by God.

Third, *some miracles to be included had not yet taken place. It would be written in God's time, not mine.* Although my nature was to accomplish, then cross off items on my "to do" list so I could move on to the next item, I must follow God's lead and His "to do" list—in His time.

Next, God said *He would establish divine relationships and arrange divine appointments through this book.* I didn't know—and still don't know—exactly what God meant by this, but His directive led me to include a contact section in the book so readers could communicate with miracle story contributors from across the globe.

Lastly God said that *through the birthing of this book, I would find a deeper intimacy with Him.* This excited me more than anything as the deepest longing of my heart was to know Him intimately. Hopeful that God would show me how to break through the Plexiglas barrier I had sensed between Him and me, I expected to discover the fullness of God for which I still hungered.

After documenting His instructions—all of which came to pass in coming months exactly as He said—I got started on what seemed like a monumental, impossible project.

Every day became a new adventure as God orchestrated miracle connections. Although still facing mounting health challenges, I responded to His leading as He crossed my path with people around the world whom He had foreordained for the miracles book. While conducting interviews and documenting God's wondrous miracles, I pressed through every day, trusting Him for strength in spite of the pain that rallied for my attention.

As I talked to people about miracles, I often quoted Psalm 77:13-14: *"What god is so great as our God? You are the God who performs miracles; You display Your power among the peoples."* This Scripture saturated times of praise and worship, enabling me to rise above my discomfort, in awe of the great God who had performed such wondrous works.

While documenting God's miracles, I continued to face trials of many kinds, often in such physical pain that I couldn't function. Refusing to surrender, I would profess aloud, "What god is so great as my God? You *are* the God who performs miracles."

In my weakest moments, I sensed the devil's taunting. "You serve a God of miracles, do you?... Where's your God now?"

But my miracle was on the way. And God was nearer than He had ever been.

For Reflection and Discussion

1. Has your Father given you a wilderness challenge? Describe your understanding of what He has asked of you, without thinking of how big or small the challenge appears to you. How do you feel about what is expected of you? Are you overwhelmed, fearful? Do you feel underqualified or ill-equipped?

2. What excuses have you used for not accepting your Father's challenge? What excuses have you made for procrastinating?

3. With notebook and pen, shut yourself in a quiet place and ask your Father for direction. What did He reveal to you? Can you embrace what He's asked of you, in spite of what you're walking through right now?

4. What steps do you need to take today to put action to His direction? Document the steps and keep it before you daily.

Reflect on what I am saying, for the Lord will give you insight into all this (2 Timothy 2:7).

Prayer of Repentance

I have made You too small in my eyes, O God. I have been blind to Your amazing, unlimited power and supernatural ability to equip me for any task. I have forgotten that Your power and Your ability reside within me because You live in me. Instead of seeing Your greatness, I've focused on my shortcomings. I see the error of my ways, Father. Forgive me for my sin, dear God. I acknowledge that I can do nothing without You, but with You, nothing is impossible.

Other areas of repentance:

Repent, then, and turn to God, so that your sins may be wiped out, that times of refreshing may come from the Lord (Acts 3:19).

Prayer of Submission

Loving Father, I'm so honored to represent You on the earth. Thank You for the privilege of being entrusted with Your work. I welcome the challenge You've given me, knowing that You have prepared me and will equip me with everything I need to get the job done. I pour out myself before You, and acknowledge my weaknesses and limitations. Fill me with more of You, Father, Your strength and Your ability. May those around me see less of me and more of You as I go forth. And may they marvel at the great things You enable me to do, giving You all glory, honor, and praise. In Jesus' name.

Other areas of submission:

Submit yourselves, then, to God (James 4:7).

My Personal Words From My Father

_____

_____

_____

Speak, Lord, for Your servant is listening (1 Samuel 3:9).

From the Father's Heart

Do you remember when My Son stood at the door of your heart and knocked? It gave me great joy when you invited Him in to dwell with you. When you invited Him, you invited Me and My Spirit, for whoever knows My Son, knows Me also. Although a mystery to you, We shall dwell with you all the days of your life. Our love, Our power, Our ability, and Our strength lies within you because of Our presence. In Us, you shall walk and live and breathe. As you trust in Our strength, you will discover the strength within you. I am your strength and you *can do* anything through Me.

Chapter 8

Special Delivery

Meditation

God has already prepared me for every assignment and provided everything I need to accomplish what He has asked of me.

Scripture Focus

For we are God's workmanship, created in Christ Jesus to do good works, which God prepared in advance for us to do (Ephesians 2:10).

What is my Father speaking to me through this Scripture?

May my meditation be pleasing to Him, as I rejoice in the Lord (Psalm 104:34).

Perseverance

When our kids were young, they'd often wake up during the night, crying from growing pains. While massaging their legs, I'd rub them down with ointment to ease their suffering. "It's OK," I'd say, trying to soothe them, "in time this, too, will pass."

Spiritual growth and development, like physical growth and development, take time and require perseverance. Growth and development—physical and spiritual—can hurt!

Prior to entering my wilderness season, I found myself nursing aching muscles after a casual three-mile walk. Physical slimness does not indicate physical fitness any more than a spiritual appearance indicates spiritual fitness.

Painfully aware of my dire need to improve my physical condition, I purposed to venture into an exercise program. After thorough fitness research, I settled on the Tae Bo video by exercise instructor Billy Blanks. Determined to give it a hearty try, I committed to doing the 30-minute workout four times a week.

The first day, I felt it best to ease into my new routine, so I sank into my comfy rocking chair and watched the video participants sweat through the program. *How could these physically fit people work up a sweat from such an easy routine?* I wondered.

The next day I joined the team in the privacy of my family room and quickly realized that the workout wasn't as easy as it appeared. Gasping for breath and writhing from sore muscles, I slumped into my recliner. Wondering if I had made a horrible mistake, I contemplated how I might wiggle out of my exercise commitment. Although tempted to eject the video and stuff it in the bottom of the closet, I pulled myself to my feet and joined back in.

What a relief to hear the instructor suggest taking a break if exercise became too difficult. Agreeing with his sound advice, I took advantage of his wise counsel and plunked back into the recliner.

By day four, I finally completed the 30-minute workout, but felt as if my life was about to expire. On day six, I determined to push through the entire routine without taking a break. I felt fine until reaching the fifth set of eight roundhouse kicks. "One more set...make it burn!" Mr. Blanks said.

"One more set?" I gasped. "Make it burn?" I wanted to fling myself to the floor and cave in to failure. Exhausted, I could barely kick my burning lead leg one more time. How I wanted to quit!

Although tempted to give up, I persevered, and eventually built physical endurance and strength that I once thought were impossible.

Before starting our journey with Christ—and venturing into the wilderness—some unknowingly assume that walking with Jesus is a cakewalk created for weaklings. Yet progressing from bystander to participant brings quick realization that a committed life in Christ is not for spiritual wimps. Following Christ—especially through desert seasons—requires strength, endurance, and a commitment to finish the race *regardless of the cost.*

The challenges of growing in spiritual maturity can tempt us to sink into our spiritual recliner, surrendering to defeat. Yet just when we think we can't hang on any longer, God steps in to refuel us. Through *His* power, *His* strength, and the victory *He* won at the cross of Calvary, we *can* persevere.

As we saw earlier in Psalm 34:19, God never promised a trouble-free life. Trial-filled wilderness walks, although challenging, are valuable tools that develop our faith muscles and keep us spiritually fit.

God can turn *any* situation around. He keeps His promises and—in His time and His way—*will* bring the victory. Our part is to persevere and believe that God will do what He promised.

Abraham, the Father of Faith, knew how to persevere. Against all hope, in hope, he believed God's promise that he would become the father of many nations. Abraham was fully persuaded that God had power to do what He had promised (see Rom. 4:18-21). God fulfilled His promise. He *always* fulfills His promises.

Are you weary from the race or exhausted from the fight of faith? As Billy Blanks says, "One more set...make it burn." Hang in there and trust God for the impossible. If you're fully persuaded that God has power to do what He promised, in the end, you will build spiritual strength and endurance to finish the race in victory.

Temptations to surrender to discouragement are Heaven-sent lessons, often sent by special delivery into the wilderness. Although you didn't order them, God's training packages will find you even if you're trying to hide. When your package arrives, you can refuse delivery and mark

"Return to Sender"—or sign for it, embracing it as an opportunity to grow.

It's wise to accept Heaven-sent packages. Rejecting God's divinely packaged lessons will only delay your wilderness journey. Because He loves you, He'll deliver lessons as many times, and in as many forms, as necessary until you receive the package and the lessons it contains.

I remember receiving my first royalty check, a Heaven-sent lesson in disguise. After tearing the envelope open, I could hardly wait to see the amount. I froze. The amount—a mere $35.99—flashed like a neon light. Knowing that most of the royalty check resulted from books I had purchased to donate, I calculated a net of $13.00, hardly enough to treat my family to a Big Mac!

"Well, Hun?" Tom joked, "I guess I'll have to wait to buy that new pickup truck."

Staring at the check, which to me indicated poor results, I felt as if the devil was awaiting my response. When God's grace enabled me to realize that the platter of discouragement set before me was a test, I determined to pass the test. As I chose to refuse the devil's tempting offer, God reminded me of something I had almost forgotten. *Obedience and faithfulness are your part*, He whispered in my heart. *The results are up to Me.*

With great joy, I sowed the royalty check, along with our tithe, into the Sunday offering. Although small, it represented more than anyone—but God—could see.

Releasing the royalties to God, I remembered a heavenly reward I had received at a women's ministry gathering a few weeks earlier. While I enjoyed breakfast with a group of women at Spokane Christian Center, Al Plue, one who had volunteered to serve the ladies asked, "How's your first book doing?"

"I don't know, Al," I said. "I haven't seen the first sales report."

Al wept, oblivious to the other women's surprise at his sudden emotion. "Several of my friends committed their lives to Jesus when they read your book," he said. "And they're attending church and men's prayer too."

"Really?" I said, adding my tears.

"I'm glad you obeyed God," Al said, wiping his cheeks.

I'm glad too!

I haven't forgotten the day God downloaded instructions for that first book into my heart. Since then He has sent my books and articles to the corners of the globe, opening doors for these writings to be translated into other languages and used in television productions. I've had the privilege of making guest appearances on programs that reached billions of people with a message of hope in Christ.

Just as God performed a miracle by multiplying some loaves of bread and a couple of fish to feed thousands, He took all I had to offer Him in the beginning—only a willingness to obey a big God who makes the impossible possible—and multiplied it to feed the multitudes with the increase He produced. Truly a miracle of multiplication! He did miracles in my life, and will do miracles in your life, because He loves people and wants them to eat of the Bread of Life.

Imagine what the disciples thought when Jesus told them to feed the 5,000, not to mention the women and children. "What? You've got to be kidding, Master! Look at all of these people. Impossible!"

The disciples rattled off the reasons they couldn't do what He had asked of them. With only five loaves of bread and two fish, how could they feed even a family of five?!

When the disciples questioned Jesus and whined about their limitations, He didn't acknowledge their lack. Instead of considering what they didn't have, He focused on what they *did* have. If all you have is a desire to obey—it's enough!

Our perceived lack does not limit God. He doesn't require a college degree, a theology degree, a perfected talent, or a perfect life to be used of Him. He doesn't expect us to have all of the answers. God doesn't reward titles or genius-level problem solving—He rewards obedience and faithfulness. *He doesn't call the qualified; He qualifies the called!* He has called you and *He* will qualify you. We would benefit by taking our focus off what we don't have and instead fix our gaze on what we *do* have, even if it's little in our sight.

As you continue your wilderness journey, God may ask what seems impossible for you. Bring the little you have to Jesus so He can bless it and multiply it. Just as He put the bread and fish back into the disciples' hands to feed the people, He will put the increase back into your hands so you can feed people from the harvest that God produces in your life. He will do it, but you must be willing and obedient to cooperate!

I encourage you right now to take time in prayer to bring what you have to God—even if it's only a willing heart. Your little—multiplied through the Master's hand—makes the impossible possible!

If you've been offered a platter of discouragement when you see what appears as poor results on a God-given assignment as I did when my puny royalty check arrived, choose to say, "Thanks, but no thanks. I'll pass!" Obedience and faithfulness are your part. *The results are up to God.*

Well, that all sure sounds nice, Therese, you might be thinking, *but you don't understand. I'm still discouraged and I still don't think I can make it!* That's wilderness talk, and if you're feeling those emotions, you're not alone. After all, it's been a long journey, and you're likely tired. God, a loving Father, knows how you feel, so don't hesitate to tell Him. He is intimately familiar with and understands our wilderness weaknesses.

If you're still thinking about giving up, hold that thought! Thomas Edison wrote, "Many of life's failures are people who did not realize how close they were to success when they gave up." Remember: your breakthrough may be right around the corner.

For Reflection and Discussion

1. Recall one of the most significant assignments your Father ever gave you. Describe the assignment and explain what you have done with it.

2. What, if anything, has hindered you from fulfilling what your Father asked of you? How do you feel about these hindrances? Talk to your Father about what you believe is holding you back. What did He reveal?

3. "Obedience and faithfulness is my part. The results are up to my Father." What does this statement mean to you?

4. What measuring stick have you used to determine the success, or failure, of God's assignments in your life? What measuring stick have you used to determine the success, or failure, of the assignments God has given your loved ones?

Reflect on what I am saying, for the Lord will give you insight into all this (2 Timothy 2:7).

Prayer of Repentance

Dear Father, giver of life, I see the ways in which I've judged myself and others for what appears as success or failure. Fear of man has proven to be a snare for me, Father. Release me from that snare, O God. Forgive me for seeking man's approval and for allowing man's opinions to guide what I do. Rise up in me, Father, and enable me to shine forth Your glory in all that I do, confidently moving forward according to Your will.

Other areas of repentance:

Repent, then, and turn to God, so that your sins may be wiped out, that times of refreshing may come from the Lord (Acts 3:19).

Prayer of Submission

Father, no longer shall I allow man's opinions to determine my success or failure. I submit to You now, and acknowledge that from this day forward, I shall stand before an audience of One. You, Father, are the One I want to please. As I obey You and remain faithful to what You've asked of me, I trust that You will bring the results You desire. Enable me to hear Your voice with clarity, and strengthen me to follow the path on which You lead. You have raised me up for such a time as this, O faithful Father, and I submit myself to You that You might have Your way in me. How I long to hear You say, "Well done, My faithful servant. Come, enter into your Father's happiness." In Jesus' name.

Other areas of submission:

Submit yourselves, then, to God (James 4:7).

My Personal Words From My Father

_____

_____

_____

Speak, Lord, for Your servant is listening (1 Samuel 3:9).

From the Father's Heart

I see everything you do, My beloved. I hear everything you say. I know the motives of your heart as I know the motives of the hearts of all people. Do not examine your life through the eyes of humankind, for human's ways are not My ways and human's thoughts are not My thoughts. People's methods of judging success and failure are not My methods. Obey Me, remain faithful to Me, and follow as I lead you on our journey together. Leave the results to Me. For then, you shall surely find great success and the abundant life I desire for you.

Chapter 9

S-T-R-E-T-C-H

Meditation

Though I do not understand what I am experiencing, and I feel overwhelmed by my circumstances, God will always be faithful to help me to endure anything and everything.

Scripture Focus

And God is faithful. He will not allow the temptation to be more than you can stand. When you are tempted, He will show you a way out so that you can endure (1 Corinthians 10:13 NLT).

What is my Father speaking to me through this Scripture?

May my meditation be pleasing to Him, as I rejoice in the Lord (Psalm 104:34).

Crying "Uncle!"

As I continued my daily trek through the wilderness terrain, God breathed into my relationship with my beloved earthly father through yet more difficult circumstances. Dad, who had been suffering from a long-term battle with prostate and bone cancer, was nearing the end of his life. Death was about to invade my wilderness season.

Daily calls and e-mails back home kept me current on Dad's deteriorating condition. I flew home to Minneapolis five times in 12 months, mostly during Dad's most critical health crisis.

The emotional strain of Dad's impending death weighed heavy; I wanted to do more to help than I was able from afar. When in Minneapolis, I felt guilty being away from Tom and the kids in Spokane; and when in Spokane, I felt guilty being unable to carry more of the load of Dad's care. I had much to learn about trusting God with my loved ones.

On one trip to Minneapolis, in God's perfect timing, He prepared Dad's heart to relocate to Our Lady of Good Counsel, a Catholic hospice home for terminal cancer patients. When my sister Janice and I crossed the threshold of this God-centered ministry, we knew in an instant that this is where Dad was supposed to be. Dad's loving heavenly Father had prepared the very best for our dad.

On Valentine's Day, our youngest son's 11th birthday, the ambulance arrived to transport Dad to the place he would spend the rest of his days.

After medical personnel loaded Dad into the ambulance, the EMT and I hopped in the back, then we started down 15th Avenue in Hopkins. Propped up on the stretcher, Dad stared out the back window through watery eyes. Fluffy snowflakes fell like a white blanket over the familiar neighborhood. Knowing Dad would never see 15th Avenue again, where he had raised his family and spent most of his married life, I stared out the back window too, trying—unsuccessfully—to hide my tears. Although relieved that Dad would receive loving care at Our Lady of Good Counsel, my heart cried over the bittersweet scene.

A fresh red rose with Valentine candy awaited Dad in his new spacious surroundings. Everything was spotless, even the air was crispy clean. God's grace poured like liquid love throughout that day, enabling me to smile through my sadness as Dad got settled.

In the coming months, I received regular updates from Janice and Jim, who spent countless hours at Dad's bedside along with a heavenly handpicked nursing staff. I'd laugh and cry at the same time, seeing the wondrous work God was doing in Dad and in those who visited Dad. The Lord orchestrated perfectly timed humorous encounters, enabling our family to chuckle in the midst of our sadness.

Dad and I shared many tender moments during my visits home that year, talking more than we had throughout my life. His eyes teared up when I held his hand and expressed my gratitude for the countless sacrifices he had made for me over the years. Words weren't necessary.

When times came to return to Spokane, I left knowing I'd likely never see Dad again until eternity. "I love you, Dad," I'd say, kissing him on the forehead before leaving.

"Love you too, Therese," he'd say, words he had previously been unable to express. Dad's expressions of love were like honey to my soul. I always stopped at his door and looked back for one last glance as if an etch-a-sketch was branding Dad's picture in my mind.

Being s-t-r-e-t-c-h-e-d between Minneapolis, Spokane, health challenges, and countless events in between, it seemed as if there was no relief in sight. And it seemed that God wasn't the slightest bit concerned about it!

I remembered, as a child, wrestling with my older brothers, Rich and Jim. They'd twist my arm behind my back, saying, "Say 'Uncle!'" Although I'd stubbornly hold off until I couldn't take it anymore, I'd eventually give in and yell, "Uncle!" so they'd release their hold on me.

Yet now when my heart cried out to God, "Uncle! Uncle! I can't do this anymore!" God didn't even acknowledge my cry of defeat. Instead, He seemed to keep right on s-t-r-e-t-c-h-i-n-g, determined to fulfill His perfect purpose in me. Though my circumstances hurt more physically, emotionally, and spiritually than my brothers' stronghold on my arm, I'm thankful that God did not release me before He accomplished what He needed to accomplish.

God seems to have no problem stretching us beyond what we likely believe are our maximum limitations, nor will He hesitate to nudge us outside of our comfort zone, prompting us to far exceed our natural strength or ability.

When God called Gideon to deliver Israel from an enemy who had ravaged them mercilessly for seven years, Gideon rattled off his lack of qualifications for the job (see Judg. 6:1-7:25). "But, Lord," Gideon asked, "how can I save Israel? My clan is the weakest in Manasseh, and I'm the least in my family." Gideon saw himself as a weakling, yet God saw him as a mighty warrior.

God sees much more in us than we see in ourselves. When He looks at us, He sees us *in Christ*. Our limited vision can only see who we are today and possibly a glimpse of what we hope to become.

God didn't acknowledge Gideon's excuses, but simply reminded him, "I will be with you." When wartime came, God stepped in and annihilated the enemy, yet not one of Gideon's small army of 300 perished. What was impossible for Gideon, God made possible.

When God called Moses to deliver Israel from the bondage of Egypt, Moses said, *"Who am I, that I should go to Pharaoh and bring the Israelites out of Egypt?"* God didn't acknowledge Moses' questions either, but assured, *"I will be with you"* (Exod. 3:11-12).

When God asks something of you, He won't launch you out on your own, although it might feel like it! As with Moses and Gideon, He may not acknowledge your complaining, but promises to be with you just as He promised to be with the men and women of faith in the Bible. He fills you with *His* ability and *His* purpose, then flows *through you* as you do *His* will.

Natural ability and strength drain quickly, but fueled with God's divine purpose and ability, we can do *all* things through Him who strengthens us (see Phil. 4:13).

As mentioned earlier, our perceived lack doesn't limit God whatsoever, nor do our weaknesses or lack of qualifications. None of it surprises God. He wants to use us in spite of ourselves! As Creator, He knows us even better than we know ourselves. Second Corinthians 12:9 says, *"My grace is sufficient for you, for My strength is made perfect in weakness"* (NKJV). When we're weak, *He* makes us strong!

Our greatest spiritual and personal growth develops as God s-t-r-e-t-c-h-e-s us. If we remain submitted to Him in our darkest and most trying times, He will bring us to a deeper faith, Christian maturity, and a greater revelation of our complete dependence on Him.

If you've been crying, "Uncle, uncle! I can't do this!" know that God is with you, just as He was with Gideon and Moses. God never gives assignments without providing the right tools to accomplish the task. He will equip you with everything you need to get the job done and will fuel you with His strength to accomplish the task.

I found myself crying "Uncle!" again one cool spring week in 2005. Between personal health trials and growing concern about Dad's deteriorating condition, I had run out of steam. Without a heavenly recharge, I felt unable to continue. Putting everything aside, I shut the world out and shut myself in with God for a prayer retreat in Blanchard, Idaho.

Several days into my time away, I took a stroll through the scenic valley. Listening to the sparrows' sweet chatter, I pondered the seeming eternity I had waited for God to deliver me from this dark season of suffering. The battle had intensified, and quitting had become an attractive option. I had been standing on God's promises for my healing and had waited for what seemed an eternity for it to come to pass. "Is it *ever* going to happen, Lord? Will I *ever* be healed?" I prayed.

Thoughts of condemnation flooded me. *Have I missed it somewhere? Is something blocking my healing? Maybe hidden sin is my problem. Possibly I haven't prayed enough. Maybe I've failed God. Is it because I haven't read the Bible enough?* Stopping abruptly on the walking trail, I hung my head in shame, not realizing the enemy had flung a net of lies over me, trying to snag me into the bottomless ravine of hopelessness.

As if God lifted my head, I looked heavenward. Perched on the highest branch of a towering tree sat a statuesque bald eagle, long used as a symbol of power, courage, and freedom.

God spoke through the silence now blanketing the valley.

They that wait upon the Lord shall renew their strength; they shall mount up with wings as eagles; they shall run, and not be weary; and they shall walk, and not faint (Isaiah 40:31 KJV).

Wait? I thought as my fleshly nature rose up. *I **have** been waiting and I'm tired of waiting!*

God understood.

"Wait," the Hebrew word *qavah*, means "to expect, patiently wait for, hope in and look for." It also means "to bind together by twisting; the extension of a cord from one point to another." "Mount up" means "to be lifted up."

Putting it together, we could say: "Those who bind themselves together with God and His Word and patiently wait for, hope in, and look for the Lord (and His promises, which are in Him!) will renew their strength. They will be lifted above their circumstances on wings like eagles. Then they will run and not be weary and will walk and not faint." Like the symbol of the eagle, power, courage, and freedom soar in Christ.

God's timing for our wilderness deliverance is rarely our preferred timing. Yet, if we remain submitted to God—while patiently waiting with hopeful expectation—more is happening than we realize. Remember, God takes us through times of testing to expose (to us) what is in our heart and to develop character, faith, and perseverance. I, like underexposed film, needed more development time!

As I continued walking through the lush valley, I recalled a note I had received from my dear friend Becky. It read:

> While I was praying for you I saw you coming out of a dark place with a bag in your hands. It contained jewels for you to give out to the Body of Christ. The Lord gave me Isaiah 45:2-3 for you. There are treasures to be found in darkness that can be found nowhere else. Take courage, Sis. You will come through this time stronger in the spirit than ever before—and in a faith rest.

Becky's note was a heavenly reminder that my wilderness season had divine purpose. I submitted myself to the Lord— again—and rejoiced in my heart, knowing that the outcome of my trial would eventually bring refreshing to others. Remembering Jesus, who "*for the joy set before Him endured the cross*" (Heb. 12:2), I refocused on the joy set before me—the fruit that would one day result from the work God was doing in me—and determined to endure.

Back in my room, I vowed to resist the temptation to come into agreement with the enemy's lies. Grabbing a scrap of paper, I wrote: "My circumstances will *never* change God or His Word, but God and His Word *will* change my circumstances."

Every God-breathed Word is unchangeable, unshakable truth; every word spoken by the devil is a lie. We must know the difference, then determine to stay in agreement with the truth—and nothing but the truth—so help us, God!

As children, if we suspected a neighborhood friend of telling a tall tale, we'd chant, "Liar, liar, pants on fire!" in unison.

Although only childhood fun, lies are nothing to laugh about. The devil, behind every lie, is a liar and the father of lies. Lying is his native language; there is *no* truth in him (see John 8:44).

A strong force damaging to the Body of Christ is the devil's lies regarding our identity in Christ. His lies, destructive and cloaked in shame, come in many varieties. "You're a loser...you're a failure...you blew it again and will never get it right...God can't use you anymore...Nobody loves you." Do those lies sound familiar?

Lies have a loud voice, especially in the wilderness where they can sound as true as a mirage can appear real.

When the enemy lies about our identity in Christ, we need our greatest offensive weapon—the Sword of the Spirit, God's Word. A child of the King of kings, full of God's purpose, wielding the Sword of the Spirit, makes all hell tremble—and silences the enemy's flapping tongue.

When the enemy says, "You can't do that!" say, "It is written, 'I can do *all* things through Christ who strengthens me!'" (see Phil. 4:13).

If the devil says, "You'll never make it through this trial!" Take out your sword and say, "It is written, 'I am *more* than a conqueror through Christ who loves me'" (see Rom. 8:37).

If the father of lies says, "You'll never be healed!" Say, "It is written, 'By the stripes of Jesus, I *am* healed! Jesus took my infirmities and bore my sicknesses'" (see Isa. 53:4; Matt. 8:17).

If the accuser says, "You really blew it this time! You're done for good and God will never use you again!" Raise your sword! "It is written, 'He works *all* things—even my mistakes—for the good of those who love Him who are called according to His purpose!'" (see Rom. 8:28).

Jesus said, *"You shall know the truth, and the truth will set you free"* (John 8:32). Take off the liar's coat of shame and put on God's robe of righteousness. Learn who you are in Christ through the Bible, then proclaim the truth of your identity in Him.

For starters, declare:

I'm a child of the King of kings, saved by grace, redeemed by the shed blood of Christ, forgiven of all sin, full of divine purpose, heir of Christ and His promises, healed and whole in Jesus' name, filled with the miracle-working power of the Holy Spirit and Heaven-bound for eternity!

You are who God says you are. And that's the truth! The next time the father of lies taunts you with his lies, hold your head high and shout, "Liar, liar, pants on fire!" Very fitting for the devil!

For Reflection and Discussion

1. What makes you feel stretched beyond your capacity? What do you feel is causing you to be stretched? What is your attitude in the midst of being stretched?

2. Have you ever experienced a trial within a trial? Explain. How did you, or are you, handling the trial?

3. If the timing of your deliverance has been different than expected, how have you felt about having to wait? Talk to your Father about having to wait.

4. What if you never see an end to your suffering? How do you feel when the outcome is different than you expected? What do you feel when the outcome seems to contradict what your Father promised you in His Word?

Reflect on what I am saying, for the Lord will give you insight into all this (2 Timothy 2:7).

Prayer of Repentance

O Lord, my gracious Father, forgive me for putting such limitations on Your ability to work in and through my life. I'm sorry for trusting in my own abilities instead of trusting in Your amazing unlimited abilities. Forgive me, loving Father, that I again forgot that I am not alone, and that I can trust You to provide everything I need for life and godliness.

Other areas of repentance:

Repent, then, and turn to God, so that your sins may be wiped out, that times of refreshing may come from the Lord (Acts 3:19).

Prayer of Submission

Father, Lord of my life, I give myself again to You, and surrender my plan to Your perfect plan. Although I feel so inadequate to accomplish what You've asked of me, I trust You to fuel me with everything I need from this day forward, to fulfill everything You desire. Without You, I can do nothing, but with You, all things are possible. In Jesus' name.

Other areas of submission:

Submit yourselves, then, to God (James 4:7).

My Personal Words From My Father

_____

_____

_____

Speak, Lord, for Your servant is listening (1 Samuel 3:9).

From the Father's Heart

Do you not know, treasured child of Mine, that My life flows through you? Do you not know that as you come to the end of yourself, that My glory shines in and through you? Let Me live through you, let Me shine in you, let My glory radiate through every part of your life in Me. For when you are unable, I am able. When you are weak, I am strong. And whatever circumstances you face, I have the answer!

Chapter 10

Dad

Meditation

Regardless of uncertain and ever-changing circumstances, my Father is in perfect control of my destiny. He and His Word will change my circumstances, but my circumstances will never change Him or His Word.

Scripture Focus

Patient endurance is what you need now, so that you will continue to do God's will, then you will receive all that He has promised (Hebrews 10:36 NLT).

What is my Father speaking to me through this Scripture?

May my meditation be pleasing to Him, as I rejoice in the Lord (Psalm 104:34).

Trial in the Midst of Trial

In May 2005 I underwent vascular stripping and ligation on both legs. Two weeks later, I traveled to Minneapolis, as hospice nurses—again—thought Dad's organs were shutting down. But Dad perked up—again—when I arrived! Every time Dad rallied, I considered it a treasured gift from God.

While in Minneapolis, I preached at Faith Christian Center Fellowship, the message focused on God's wondrous miracles. Pain pulsating down my legs intensified as I ministered and encouraged the congregation to trust God for miracles and release their faith in spite of the circumstances they might be facing.

I sensed the taunting of darkness whispering, "Great example you are of God's miracles! God obviously didn't heal you...you had to have surgery...you're in pain...looks like your great God of miracles forgot about you!"

In spite of the demonic opposition, I preached God's Word with boldness, sharing the wondrous miracles God was doing in the earth. His power *is* strongest when we are weak! (See Second Corinthians 12:9.)

When Dad stabilized, I returned to Spokane and sought medical attention as my post-surgical leg pain had become unbearable. After seeing several surgeons, it was determined that I was experiencing a foreign body reaction to the internal sutures, a common surgical material.

When physical discomfort worsened and incisions did not improve, the surgeon reopened the incisions and removed the suture material. "Those are some of the angriest wounds I've ever seen," he said. "Your body won't tolerate this stuff and will fight it until it's out of your body."

Once the material was excised, the incisions healed with no further complications. "If you ever require surgery in the future," the surgeon sternly warned me on a follow-up visit, "be certain to warn medical staff that you can't have Vicryl sutures. There are many other suture options, so it shouldn't be a problem." I wholeheartedly agreed!

Two months after vascular surgery, I was scheduled for a complete hysterectomy. Because of my previous surgical complications, I advised medical personnel of my allergy-like suture reaction, taking extreme measures to ensure my safety in surgery. The memory still fresh of having my leg incisions reopened, my stomach tightened at the thought of what might happen if the surgeon used the wrong material. I fought visions of my abdomen being reopened to excise multiple layers of sutures required for this major surgery. "I don't know what type of sutures you use," I told medical staff, "but please *don't* use Vicryl!"

I notified my surgeon's office and the hospital in advance to ensure the suture information was included in my records and advised nurses and anesthesiologists on the day of surgery regarding my body's suture response. In response, hospital staff secured a bright pink allergy band on my wrist that read "VICRYL SUTURE ALLERGY" in bold black lettering.

In the pre-op area, surrounded by hospital staff and Tom, the surgeon reviewed standard surgical questions. "Do you have any allergies?" he asked.

"No medication allergies, but I'm definitely allergic to Vicryl sutures," I told him.

I explained my recent experience after vascular surgery, offering to show him my still-healing incision sites from the previous surgery.

"I've done thousands of surgeries using this suture material," he said, "and I've never had trouble with it before."

As he spoke, I saw PRIDE written on his forehead, as if a piece of information had been dropped into my mind.

"But I *do* have trouble with it," I said, then medical staff wheeled me into surgery.

It would be weeks before I learned that in spite of my repeated warnings and requests, the surgical team had used Vicryl sutures.

Other than some difficulty in pain control, initial post-surgical recovery was non-eventful. Several weeks later, however, when the internal sutures should begin to dissolve as they do in most cases, my body reacted as it did after the previous vascular surgery. Fever, swollen abdomen, and intense pain landed me in the emergency room where I soon learned that the dreaded suture material laced my insides.

Each step I took required a concentrated effort to control my breathing, as each breath and every movement sent me through the roof in pain. To control the foreign body reaction raging in my abdomen, an IV pick was inserted in my arm for repeated hour-long antibiotic infusions. "Help me, God" became my moment by moment cry. Although it seemed unbearable, God did help me moment by moment.

My imagination strayed. As thoughts of the horror of suture removal tortured me, I battled a spirit of fear. I feared additional surgery. I feared pain. And I feared death.

Because of the high risk involved in reopening my abdomen to locate and excise several layers of suture material, doctors opted to keep me on long-term painkillers until the material eventually dissolved. All I could do was wait and take a day at a time.

It made no sense to me. We had prayed and believed God for protection in surgery. We had asked Him to grant wisdom to the surgeon and his team. *Didn't God hear?* I wondered. *Didn't He care?*

God had heard. And He did care. But for now, remembering that His ways were not my ways, I chose to trust Him in spite of my lack of understanding. Feeling as if I were drowning, I grabbed on to Jesus and floated.

In August of that year, still suffering from the consequences of the surgical error made during my hysterectomy, I was recovering from yet another surgery to remove a schwannoma nerve tumor from my left leg. My circumstances continued to make no sense whatsoever. Instead of improving, I had grown worse. Instead of pain decreasing, it had increased. My body was tired of fighting. And so was I.

Because I had been laid up for an extended time and realized that the kids had little opportunity for summer activities, I took them and their friends to Silverwood and Boulder Beach in Northern Idaho.

After the kids scurried into the water park, I sank into my lounge chair, grabbed a magazine, and hoped to soak in an afternoon of much-needed sunshine and rest.

But God had another plan.

Glancing at the sea of people, my attention settled on a woman sitting across the water park.

As if God had pulled the woman out of the crowd with a people magnifying glass, she came into focus. *Do you see her?* the Lord seemed to whisper.

Yes, Lord, I see her, I answered in my heart.

I love her and want to touch her. Seeing her through His eyes, I sensed some measure of the depth of God's unconditional love and deep desire to touch her life.

Later, my attention was drawn to a young man lounging at poolside, his large tattooed body hard to miss. *Do you see him?* the Lord seemed to ask.

I see him, Lord.

I love him and want to touch him. My heart swelled with God's divine love and compassion for this man.

Throughout the day, the Lord continued to highlight people of all sizes, shapes, ages, and colors. They seemed nothing out of the ordinary, except that God had pointed them out and enabled me to sense His tangible love for each one.

I never got around to reading my magazine that day, but I left the park with a deeper revelation of God's longing for people to know His unfailing love. But my wilderness lessons weren't over yet, as I still didn't understand the depth of God's love for *me*.

I felt so alone, even in crowds. Hearing others laughing and enjoying life seemed odd. And I was scared, wondering what the future held for my family and me. When previous surgical error resulted in continued suffering, I wondered if I might die prematurely, leaving my children without a mother. The physical battle lingered on with no end in sight, making weary discouragement my daily bread.

I wanted to throw in the towel more times than I can recall; I didn't feel I could muster the physical or emotional strength to persevere. Although Tom, the kids, and several dear friends offered support and encouragement, nothing seemed to help me feel better.

Adding to my burden, I was concerned about how my suffering was affecting my loved ones. Each, in their own way, were working through my circumstances and processing their own thoughts of what the future might hold for me—and for them.

By November, Dad's bone cancer progressed, leaving his legs useless. I flew to Minneapolis again, cherishing another opportunity to share time with Dad. On Thanksgiving, we planned to gather at the hospice, hoping to enjoy the holiday dinner around Dad's bed. When we arrived, however, we found Dad sitting up in the recliner chair, smiling, with a twinkle in his eye!

Using a crane-like contraption, the caring nurses had lifted Dad into the chair for this special occasion. Sister Jane, Mom's sister, my sister Janice and her husband Mike, my brother Jim, Dad, and I enjoyed the most memorable day of gratitude! The Thanksgiving Day delicacies tasted like manna from Heaven and the aroma of love freshened the air.

The following February word came that Dad was at the end. Although I had received calls like this before, and my sister and I had even kidded about the many false alarms, I sensed in my heart that Dad's time to go to his eternal home had arrived.

When I arrived in Minneapolis, February 25, 2006, Dad had been in and out of consciousness, then entered a coma-like state. Sitting at his bedside I wondered what was going on inside Dad's heart. *Was he reflecting on his life? Was he talking to God? Did he have any regrets? Did he know how much I loved him?* I was grateful that the hospice staff allowed me to stay at Dad's side around the clock, as I didn't want to leave him. I didn't want him to die alone.

After several days and nights, Dad suddenly sat up in bed early one morning and looked at me with a grin. "Let's get this show on the road," he said.

I smiled, remembering how Dad had often used that phrase when trying to get our young family out the door, especially on Sundays when he didn't want to be late for church. It seemed as if Dad had settled things within himself and was ready to meet Jesus.

Dad died March 5, 2006. Our loss was surely Heaven's gain!

For Reflection and Discussion

1. Reflect on a time when you were wronged by someone who either didn't realize they had wronged you, or who had refused to acknowledge their wrong. What was your response at the time? How do you feel about it now?

2. In response to question 1, talk to your Father about unresolved feelings you might have toward your offender or others involved. Make the choice to forgive, even if you don't feel like forgiving. Your Father will help you through the process. Release the person, and the situation, to your Father.

3. Think about your relationship with your earthly father. Do you have any unresolved issues with your earthly father? Explain.

4. Spend time with your heavenly Father to talk about your earthly father. Rejoice with thanks for the good memories and surrender the disappointments and sad memories. Ask your Father to use all, good and not so good, for your good and for His glory. Pray a blessing over your father and thank your heavenly Father for him.

Reflect on what I am saying, for the Lord will give you insight into all this (2 Timothy 2:7).

Prayer of Repentance

Everlasting Father, I have sinned against You and against others. I received Your forgiveness, yet have been unwilling to forgive others as You have forgiven me. I'm sorry for holding bitterness and unforgiveness toward those who have wronged me in the past. I'm sorry for blaming You and questioning You for allowing painful experiences in my life. I'm sorry, my wondrous Creator, for the judgments I've held against my earthly father for actions that only You understand. I choose to forgive my father. I choose to forgive my offenders, Lord God, and ask that You not hold their actions against them. As You have released me from the punishment of sin, I ask that You release them too.

Other areas of repentance:

Repent, then, and turn to God, so that your sins may be wiped out, that times of refreshing may come from the Lord (Acts 3:19).

Prayer of Submission

Father, the darkness in my heart caused my heart to be far from You, but praise Your holy name, You have wiped away my iniquities and have washed away my sin! There is much that I don't understand, Father, much has happened that makes no sense to me, but I trust that nothing touched my life without Your knowledge. Bless my earthly father, Father God, bless those who have harmed me in the past. May Your finest blessing chase them down and overtake them! I have chosen to forgive as You have forgiven me. Help me now, Father, through the process of healing. In Jesus' name.

Other areas of submission:

Submit yourselves, then, to God (James 4:7).

My Personal Words From My Father

_____

_____

_____

Speak, Lord, for Your servant is listening (1 Samuel 3:9).

From the Father's Heart

All of Heaven rejoices as you forgive! All of Heaven rejoices as you choose to release My love through forgiveness. I have wiped out your sin, and now pour out upon you a time of refreshing. Receive the refreshing wind of My Spirit as We blow through your heart, mind, body, and soul. My healing power is flowing. Receive. Sit before Me now, and don't hasten our time together. For the great work I am doing in and through you will change you forever. The wounds I am healing in you, I shall use to bring healing to others. Vessel of My love, let Me fill you to the fullest, that you might pour out and come back for more.

Chapter 11

The Secret Chamber

Meditation

I can hide nothing from my Father. He sees everything in me and knows every secret I have hidden in my heart.

Scripture Focus

If we had forgotten the name of our God or spread our hands in prayer to foreign gods, God would surely have known it, for He knows the secrets of every heart (Psalm 44:20-21 NLT).

What is my Father speaking to me through this Scripture?

May my meditation be pleasing to Him, as I rejoice in the Lord (Psalm 104:34).

Hidden Areas of the Heart

When our son James moved out during his high school senior year, it tore my heart and magnified my grief. The strained relationship between Tom and James, a significant burden I had carried in silence for 15 years, had climaxed. I hated the anger, I hated the tension, and I hated that Tom and James appeared to hate each other. Worst of all, I hated that I couldn't fix it.

Desperate, I sought counseling with Dave Hutchins of the Genesis Institute, a man who considered himself a spiritual mentor. I liked that term better than "counselor" as it soothed my flawed skeptical attitude that counselors were perceived as being for mentally unstable or weak people who couldn't cope on their own.

I headed to the Genesis Institute certain that my purpose was to fix my family, or at least to learn how to survive! Before the end of the first session, however, it became obvious that God didn't bring me there to fix my family. He had work to do in *me*.

Dave seemed stunned when I shared my history. "The things you're telling me are tragic," he said, "yet you talk about them like a reporter reporting the news. You don't express one ounce of emotion. You're here in this office, but your emotions are somewhere in the next building—maybe even down the block!"

Dave recognized something to which I was blind: I had detached from my emotions. "I can't make myself feel emotions that don't exist," I said, not understanding his comments. "That's just the way things were. I don't have emotions about it."

I soon learned that emotions did exist, but because I had stuffed them so deep in my heart, it would take time for them to surface. God's time.

Men, Dave explained, often react in anger to painful experiences, but repress the hurt emotions. Women, he said, do the opposite, often reacting initially with hurt emotions, but repressing the anger. Hurt and anger that have been pushed down simmer below the surface until they eventually surface.

Although I believed what Dave said to be true, I couldn't relate on a personal level, oblivious to the anger simmering in my heart like a volcano ready to blow. "I don't have any anger that I'm aware of," I told him.

"Yes, you *do* have anger," Dave said. "A lot of anger." His comment bewildered me, but I didn't know that anger, and other fragile emotions, were still trapped deep in the secret chamber of my heart.

Although uncomfortable talking about my feelings, I was determined—and desperate—to follow God as He led. *"Forgetting those things which are behind"* (Phil. 3:13 KJV) had been branded on my heart through unbalanced spiritual teaching, therefore my belief system rebelled against dredging up the past. I soon realized, however, that God was taking me into the past to heal areas of my heart so I could move forward. In time, healing tears watered my dry soul and buds of fruitfulness sprouted.

Physical challenges continued a downward spiral, each swirl bringing more symptoms and an array of medications to treat those symptoms. The fibro fog enveloped me daily, making it impossible to concentrate on simple tasks. When I tried to read the Bible, I'd reread the same paragraph again and again, unable to grasp or understand what I was reading. Frustrated, I couldn't remember the hundreds of Scriptures I had previously memorized. I felt like a miserable failure as a Christian, not living up to the standard I believed God expected of me.

One day, my body wracked with pins and needles pain while I lay in the recliner, it seemed as if a black cloud had settled over my body, soul, and spirit. God was nowhere to be found and quite frankly, I was tired of playing hide and seek! I had lost my normally disciplined prayer life and when I could muster enough strength to pray, Heaven felt like brass. My Bible sat on the coffee table, most days unopened.

Alone and frightened, I wondered what tomorrow might bring. Needing an emotional embrace that no human could offer, I longed to ask God to comfort me, but hesitated, fearing He wouldn't respond. Although I didn't want to face rejection, desperation drove me to risk it.

I bowed my head. "Father," I prayed, "Would You comfort me? I'm scared and I feel so alone. I need to know You're here with me."

Heaven responded with silence, kicking my "auto reject" into gear. I unconsciously deposited another perceived rejection in the secret chamber of my heart, closed my Bible, and left the room as if nothing had happened.

I might mention that I had only waited a few seconds before determining that God had rejected me. After all, He had more important things on His plate than my childish need for comfort.

I tried to move on, but the more I thought about God ignoring me, the more I sensed unrest in my soul. Anger rose like emotional lava.

Because of the work God had been doing in the wilderness, instead of burying the perceived rejection as I had done all my life, I pondered my feelings. It bothered me that the first time I asked God to comfort me, He didn't even give me a simple sign that He was there! No warm fuzzy. Nothing. That hurt! And it made me mad.

At my next meeting with Dave I shared my experience. "What did you do when God didn't seem to respond to your request for comfort?" he asked.

"I closed my Bible and went on with my day," I said, not thinking anything of it.

"Next time, wait," Dave encouraged. "If you'll wait, God will take you where He wants to lead you."

Although highly uncomfortable, I followed Dave's suggestion. "Father, please comfort me," I asked. This time, although I wanted to bolt as my "auto reject" tried to engage, I waited. And I waited. And waited. The familiar silence shouted, invoking great discomfort. How I wanted to flee!

Feeling as if I had stepped into spiritual quicksand, I opened my eyes and tried to focus. A handwritten paper in my Bible, which was opened to the Psalms, reflected my heart expressed through King David:

O Lord, why do You stand so far away? Why do You hide when I am in trouble?...Why have You abandoned me?

Why are You so far away when I groan for help?...Why have You tossed me aside? Why must I wander in grief oppressed by my enemies? (Psalm 10:1; 22:1; 43:2, NLT)

"Why, God?" I asked. "Why?" God remained silent. "Why won't You comfort me, God?" I cried. "Am I not *good* enough for You? Haven't I *done* enough for You? Haven't I *prayed* enough? Don't You *love* me?"

I wondered if lightning bolts might strike me dead, but nothing happened. As I waited in His silent presence, sudden tears welled, then dripped into my lap.

Without knowing it, I had invited God into the secret chamber of my heart marked "Keep Out." In that chamber, I had developed a warped belief system that could be summarized in four words: "God doesn't love me." When I allowed God to open that door, a flood of tears broke like a dam as God reviewed my life like an old time picture show.

Pouring out my heart to God, one question led to another and one memory led to another. That day, and in days to come, God took me back to my childhood and walked me forward. I wasn't praying or studying, only sitting with Him and allowing Him to review life experiences that had wounded me.

I recalled being tall and lanky as a teen, secretly dreaming of a modeling career. After responding to a "models wanted" newspaper ad, I begged Dad to drive me to the interview. Dad agreed.

Dressed in my Sunday best, I headed to downtown Minneapolis with Dad. My eyes widened as we pulled into the parking lot. Every window of the building had been painted black. Fear gripped me as a lump appeared in my throat. "Are you *sure* this is the right address?" I asked.

"This is it," Dad said, double-checking the address.

Although hesitant, I gingerly stepped into the black building while Dad waited in the car.

A black leather vested man gave me the once over when I came through the door. "Are you Therese?" he asked, eyeing me from head to toe again.

"Yes," I said.

"Nice name," he said. "Follow me." After he led me into a large mirror-walled room, I scanned my surroundings. Seeing only a boom box, my heart raced. "I'll give you a few minutes to get out of your clothes," he said. "Then we'll get started." He shot me a grin, took a long drag off his cigarette, then pulled the door shut behind him.

I froze. *Take my clothes off?* I thought. Seeing the boom box, I realized that the models they were interviewing were not modeling the latest fashions.

The leather clad man returned, finding me fully clothed in the same spot he had left me. "Is there a problem?" he asked.

Unsure of how to respond, I hesitated. "I can't take my clothes off."

Looking me over again, he asked, "How old *are* you?"

"Fifteen."

His face paled. Wasting no time, he escorted me out of the ebony building. "You better leave right now," he said, shooing me out the door. "Come back when you're legal."

Dad never asked me what happened inside that building. And I never said a word.

A lie took root in my heart when I entered that dark environment alone that day: *Dad won't protect me from danger, and therefore I'm not safe.* And later, that lie became, *God won't protect me from danger, and therefore I'm not safe.*

Sitting in God's presence, I mourned the frightened teen who had walked into that shady building, not knowing what she might face. But I realized that Jesus had accompanied me into the building that day.

As I sat silently, God led me back to school gatherings, concerts, and other special events that Dad didn't attend. I remembered high school graduation where Dad was noticeably absent when I walked across the stage to receive my diploma. A lie established itself deeper at each event: *I'm not important to Dad.* And later, that lie became *I'm not important to God.*

I wept, allowing myself to experience the 18-year-old young lady's disappointment of longing for, but not seeing her dad in those audiences. But I realized that Jesus had attended every activity like a proud papa, sitting in the audience witnessing and enjoying every minute.

I couldn't remember having a conversation with Dad. Not one. Although I didn't understand why Dad didn't talk to me, I understood the false message it stamped on my heart: *Dad isn't interested in me or my life.* Later, I translated that lie, *God isn't interested in me or my life.*

I grieved over the young girl who wanted her dad to ask her about school, boys, and future dreams. Jesus had been there though, always available for intimate conversations and interested in every detail of my life, big and small.

Anxious to bring home report cards, I worked diligently throughout grade school to earn perfect grades. When Dad didn't acknowledge my flawless school reports, another lie took hold: *Dad isn't proud of me,* which later I interpreted as *God isn't proud of me.*

I cried over the schoolgirl who hungered to hear, "I'm proud of you!" But I smiled through those tears, knowing Jesus had been there, rejoicing and radiating with pride at the good report.

As we reviewed my life together, I continued to ask God questions that I'd always been afraid to ask. I expressed emotions that had been bottled up as God did an emotional purging and a spiritual cleansing.

I knew in my heart that my lack of understanding wasn't Dad's fault whatsoever. I sensed overwhelming love and compassion for Dad, who had been plagued by and suffered from depression. God used Dave to help me realize, however, that although there were valid reasons for Dad's inability to express the love God desired for him to give his children, the fact was, I had suffered as a result—as millions across the globe—young and old—have suffered when lacking their earthly father's expression of God's love.

As God invaded the secret chamber that I had so carefully guarded all my life, He exposed the lies I had believed about myself and shined the light of His Word. As the Truth permeated my heart, His light extinguished the darkness and eradicated the enemy's lies.

A transformation took place in my darkest hour. As God's love drove out fear and the light of His Word swallowed up the lies of darkness, a wondrous truth started to settle in my heart: *God loves and cherishes me!* He had walked with me, His treasured daughter, since the beginning, through the good times and the not-so-good times.

I was beginning to get it! God's love was not based on what I did—or didn't do—for Him. I couldn't work or earn my way to His love. God was breaking the defective performance thermometer I had used throughout my life to measure my worth in His sight. I was born the King's daughter but had been living as a spiritually orphaned pauper!

I had previously taught on Hebrews 13:5 (NKJV): *"I will never leave you nor forsake you"* explaining that "never," the Greek word *ou may*, means "by no means, never, in no way, nor ever, under *no* circumstances." With great boldness, I'd say, "God will never, never, never, ever, ever, ever, by no means, never, in no way, not ever, under *no* circumstances, leave you!"

At the height of my wilderness suffering, I'd personalize the promise by faith, saying, "In spite of how I feel, God promised He'd never leave me or forsake me, so I believe He's here even if doesn't feel like He's here." Now, these words—by faith—became divine revelation as I saw God's presence in and through my pain.

At times, God seems to withdraw from us. Yet, even His apparent withdrawal has purpose. Second Chronicles 32:31 says that God healed Hezekiah, then tested his character by withdrawing—to expose what was really in his heart.

God may seem to withdraw from us in the wilderness too, testing us to expose—to us—what is in our hearts. Our heart condition never surprises God, who already knows the heart of every man and woman. But as He exposes our heart condition to *us,* He also provides opportunities to respond to, and correct, anything needing adjustment.

When we can't sense God's presence and Heaven seems silent, the test can be grueling—and lonely. It requires faith to believe God is there when it feels like He has not only abandoned us, but has left no forwarding address!

First Corinthians 10:13 says that God *"will not let you be tempted beyond what you can bear"* and that *"when you are tempted, He will also provide a way out so that you can stand up under it."* Temptation, which means "testing," reveals true character.

When you're thrown in the pressure cooker and pressed on every side, surface goodness can fade as other parts of our yet undeveloped character arise to be exposed for all—including us—to see. The bad news is that rough edges surface when we're squeezed. The good news is that God will help smooth those rough edges!

God's testing and apparent withdrawal exposed the lies that had blocked me from receiving the Father's love. Lacking a revelation of God's love would have forever hindered me from trusting or resting in Him. Exposing, confronting, and squelching the lies the enemy had sown throughout my life led to deliverance and victory. And it will for you too! As you learn the truth, the truth will set you free!

For Reflection and Discussion

1. Reflect on your life. Have you developed a secret chamber in your heart where you've stored painful or unresolved issues? What have you done with feelings during your most painful life experiences?

2. Are you willing to invite God into the secret chamber of your heart? Tell Him what you believe might be in there. If you are not aware of a secret chamber in your heart, will you give your Father permission to reveal hidden areas that He wants to expose? Take time to talk to Him about what you're feeling right now.

3. Make a list of the hurts you've stored in your heart. Make a date with your Father to talk to Him about each one, even if it takes an extended time. Ask Him to take you to those places needing healing.

4. Describe what happened when you opened the door to your secret chamber. What did your Father reveal to you?

Reflect on what I am saying, for the Lord will give you insight into all this (2 Timothy 2:7).

Prayer of Repentance

Lord God, I'm weighed down and weary after trying to carry my burdens by myself instead of giving them to You. I confess that I've often run to others for help instead of running to You. I'm sorry for trying to hide my pain from You. I've worn a mask, thinking I could hide my true feelings from You instead of openly sharing my feeling with You. Forgive me, Father, cleanse me of my sin and make me white as snow once again.

Other areas of repentance:

Repent, then, and turn to God, so that your sins may be wiped out, that times of refreshing may come from the Lord (Acts 3:19).

Prayer of Submission

Oh, God, I bow before You, maker of Heaven and earth. I come boldly before Your throne of grace to receive mercy and grace in my time of need. I bare my soul to You, sovereign God, and invite You to stir the deep waters of my soul. I'm taking my mask off, and want to show You who I am, though You already know. Open my eyes, and show me what I need to see, Father. In Jesus' name.

Other areas of submission:

Submit yourselves, then, to God (James 4:7).

My Personal Words From My Father

_____

_____

_____

Speak, Lord, for Your servant is listening (1 Samuel 3:9).

From the Father's Heart

My beloved, I marvel as you share your fragile secrets with Me. You shall see, My child, that I have been by your side through all you have walked through since the day of your birth. Do you not know that I have collected every tear you've shed? As we review your life together, past, present, and future, I shall touch your wounds with My healing balm and will turn your mourning into joy.

Chapter 12

Have No Fear

Meditation

I have no reason to fear, because my Father is with me. I am safe under the shadow of His wing.

Scripture Focus

So do not fear, for I am with you; do not be dismayed, for I am your God. I will strengthen you and help you; I will uphold you with My righteous right hand (Isaiah 41:10).

What is my Father speaking to me through this Scripture?

May my meditation be pleasing to Him, as I rejoice in the Lord (Psalm 104:34).

Love, Trust, and Rest

Pain accompanied me daily, as my health continued to deteriorate. Although my circumstances remained unchanged, God continued to change *me* in my circumstances. God, in His great wisdom, continued leading me on the perfect wilderness path to discover His love at a deeper level of intimacy—even if that path would be painful.

Although I had initially resisted God's "time out" as most children do, God used it as a tool to get me where I needed to go. Suffering had become the norm, but eventually took a back seat to the supernatural work unfolding in me. As revelation of God's love increased, I trusted Him in a greater measure, and as I trusted Him in a greater measure, I was finding rest! Trusting Him—knowing He was in control of my life and believing that nothing would come into my life without being filtered through Him first—fostered increasing rest in my soul.

As my friend Delsie once said, "Some things can't be taught; they have to be caught." I was catching God's love. I was getting it! *Because He loved me,* I believed He would protect me. *Because He loved me,* I believed He would not want any harm to come to me. *Because He loved me,* I believed He would always do what is best for me—even if it hurt! Knowing that because God knew what I was facing and knew what was best, *everything* was going to be OK, in spite of tumultuous circumstances.

Trust, rest, and knowing God's love are like a three-strand cord that, if intact, cannot be broken. If we know God's love, we can trust Him—and if we trust Him, we can find rest in Him.

One hurdle, however, had yet to be overcome: Fear of death.

Although I knew I would spend eternity with God in Heaven, I felt troubled about the possibility of leaving the kids motherless and Tom a widower.

I wrestled with God for several months while mentally battling thoughts regarding a potential untimely death. "By the stripes of Jesus, I'm healed," I'd say out loud, trying to convince myself that a premature death couldn't be possible. "With *long* life God will satisfy me" (see Isa. 53:5; Ps. 91:16).

"But...," the voice of the enemy echoed through my thoughts like poison arrows, "What about Patty Durgan...what about Peggy Tipton...what about the others who stood in faith for healing, yet died prematurely? That Scripture stuff didn't work for them."

I spent countless hours wrestling with these questions for which I found no easy answer. In fact, I found no answer at all. Yet God reminded me—again—that I couldn't establish my faith based on other people's experience, but had to stand on my own faith. Only God knew the details of Peggy's and Patty's and the others' lives and hearts—I didn't. Though I didn't understand what I had determined were premature deaths, I had to believe God for my own life.

Instead of trying to figure out what I didn't understand, I purposed to stand firm on what I did understand. I *did* know that God cannot lie (see Titus 1:2). I *did* know that Jesus paid a great price for my healing (see Isa. 53:3-5). I *did* know that He promised to satisfy me with long life (see Ps. 91:16). I *did* know that His Word was forever settled in Heaven (see Ps. 119:89).

If God said it, I believed it, and that settled it—once and for all!

With a greater awareness of God's sovereignty, and a deeper understanding of my inability to know God's ways, I found peace regarding death. I knew that, if for a reason beyond my understanding, God took me to my eternal home early, it would be best. His love only allows what is best. If I died, He would care for my children and husband, as He loved them even more than I did.

I still didn't understand my circumstances and couldn't figure out the details, but I believed that *God* understood the circumstances and *He* would figure out the details. God had allowed this wilderness season for a divine purpose greater than I could understand and whatever He desired was agreeable to me.

Releasing all to Him—again—my desires were set on knowing Him. My healing, my wilderness breakthrough, everything else—took a back seat to the pursuit of my loving Father. The apostle Paul's words rang in my spirit: *"I consider everything a loss compared to the surpassing greatness of knowing Christ Jesus my Lord"* (Phil. 3:8).

Fear of death no longer had a death grip on me. My name was written in the Lamb's book of life, and I, therefore, would spend eternity with God! If I never breathed another breath, that *alone* was more than enough.

Fear of all kinds runs rampant, even in the Body of Christ. Wars and rumors of wars splash across television screens and newspapers, leaving young and old alike numbing themselves with drugs and alcohol, then tossing and turning during sleepless nights. Worry consumes anxious thoughts as taunting questions play like a broken record, especially in the darkness of wilderness seasons when silence screams like a clanging symbol.

While witnessing terror-filled atrocities whose tentacles reach the corners of the globe, one can wonder where God is in the midst of it all.

God repeatedly says in His Word, "Fear not!" Yet, with daily tragedy splattered on the nightly news, how can one avoid being consumed with fear?

When I was a child, we traveled to southern Minnesota to visit my uncle's farm during the sweltering summer months. Stretches of farm country surrounded the little log cabin where we made our temporary abode.

Late one afternoon, the sky blackened. Seeing the monstrous storm closing in, I scampered to Uncle John's rustic log cabin for cover. The other adults' stoic faces magnified the fear already gripping my heart as images of our log cabin flying through the air, like Dorothy's house in the *Wizard of Oz*, filled my imagination.

After grabbing food and water, Dad led us outside to an underground cellar built to protect people during storms. Fighting gale force winds, he lifted the heavy wooden cover, then we crept down the cold cement stairs, trying to avoid the ornate spider webs lacing the vault-like room. We lit candles, then waited in silence.

Frozen with fear, I listened as the tornado-like blast left its fingerprint above ground. After announcing its outburst of anger, nature's storm lifted into the heavens as if it had changed its mind.

The wind stopped; all was still. Dad pushed the lid open and we climbed into the light to find devastated crops, toppled trees, and damaged farm buildings. Evidence of the storm's destructive force surrounded us, yet we were unharmed, safely nestled in the protective shelter—thanks to Dad and to God!

Likewise, God keeps us safe in His secret hiding place, the shelter and covering He designed for us. When life's storms rage, we can rest, hidden in God's protective secret place.

The Israelites witnessed God's hand of protection when the plagues of judgment fell on Egypt. Because Pharaoh refused to let God's people go, various plagues devastated the Egyptians. The Israelites, however, remained untouched in the midst of peril (see Exod. 8–12).

When the plague of livestock swept through the land, all of the Egyptians' livestock—but *not one* animal belonging to the Israelites—died. The plague of festering boils covered *only* the Egyptians.

The plague of hail struck everything in the fields, *except* in Goshen, where the Israelites were. The plague of total darkness covered Egypt for three days, yet the Israelites enjoyed light where they lived.

God's final blow struck down every firstborn of Egypt. But God instructed His people to put the blood of a perfect lamb on the top and sides of their doorframes. The death angel, seeing the sacrificial lamb's blood, passed over God's people.

As the blood of the lamb protected Israel from the death angel, the blood of Jesus, the perfect sacrificial Lamb of God, protects us, or causes disaster to pass over us. Rushing calamities will not touch one hiding under the protective covering of God.

A thousand may fall at your side, ten thousand at your right hand, but it will not come near you. You will only observe with your eyes and see the punishment of the wicked (Psalm 91:7-8).

You may see the devastation, just as the Israelites saw the devastating plagues upon Egypt, but it will not come near you.

As you trust God, fear will dissipate as you rest under the shadow of His wing. Then, as David wrote, you can say of the Lord, *"He is my refuge and my fortress, my God in whom I trust"* (Ps. 91:2).

For Reflection and Discussion

1. What is the relationship between your ability to trust your Father and your ability to receive His love? In what ways can you learn to trust Him and receive His love at a deeper level?

2. Do you believe that the Bible is your Father's personal Word to you? Do you believe the Bible is the

unchanging Word of Truth or do you only believe certain portions of Scripture that you find most easy to understand or believe? Explain your exposure to the Bible and your attitudes about it throughout your life.

3. Is your faith based on your experiences and your observations of others or is it based on God's written Word? Share examples to explain. What does "walk by faith and not by sight" mean to you? By which are you walking?

4. First John 4:18 says, *"There is no fear in love. But perfect love drives out fear, because fear has to do with punishment. The one who fears is not made perfect in love."* How does a greater revelation of your Father's love drive fear from your life?

Reflect on what I am saying, for the Lord will give you insight into all this (2 Timothy 2:7).

Prayer of Repentance

Lord God, I have failed to take You at Your Word. Like the waves of the sea, I have allowed my circumstances to toss me to and fro. I want to set my feet on Your solid foundation, Father. Fear has gripped my heart, and my faith has wavered. Instead of trusting You, I've put my trust in sinking sand. As I close doors to doubt and unbelief, I open the door to Your Truth. As I read Your Word, give me wisdom, O God, give me revelation so I might know You and Your ways. Impart to me a greater revelation of Your unfailing love, and teach me to trust You in all things. Help me to write Your Word on the tablet of my heart, Lord, and let it guide me through the uncertain times in the wilderness.

Other areas of repentance:

Repent, then, and turn to God, so that your sins may be wiped out, that times of refreshing may come from the Lord (Acts 3:19).

Prayer of Submission

Loving Lord, I come to sit at Your feet. Teach me Your ways; teach me Your Word. You know the most effective ways to teach me how to walk by faith. Open my spiritual eyes that I might see beyond my changing circumstances to focus on Your promises. I want to know Your love, my Lord, but can learn nothing without Your Spirit. Take my hand, Father God, and show me the way to a deeper love. Fill me with Your love, and drive every remnant of fear far from me so I can trust You and rest in You. In Jesus' name.

Other areas of submission:

Submit yourselves, then, to God (James 4:7).

My Personal Words From My Father

_____

_____

_____

Speak, Lord, for Your servant is listening (1 Samuel 3:9).

From the Father's Heart

Oh yes, My child! You shall know My love! And My love will bring great liberty and freedom to every fiber of your being. To know Me and My love, you must know My Son, and to know My Son, you must know My Word. For in the beginning was the Word, and the Word was with Me and the Word was Me. My Son became flesh and dwelled among you (see John 1:1-14). It is a mystery! You shall learn My love, cherished one of Mine, as you sit at My feet, as you soak in My written Word, and as you walk with Me, My Son, and My Spirit.

Chapter 13

Available

Meditation

As I pour myself into others, my Father pours into me.

Scripture Focus

A generous man will prosper; he who refreshes others will himself be refreshed (Proverbs 11:25).

What is my Father speaking to me through this Scripture?

May my meditation be pleasing to Him, as I rejoice in the Lord (Psalm 104:34).

Refreshing and Being Refreshed

One morning, I lay in bed after another restless night. Registering 11 on a pain scale of 1-10, I would have given almost anything to pull the covers over my head and wallow in self-pity. Because Tom was traveling on business—as he did about 60 percent of the time—and much-needed household errands had accumulated, I had to forgo the pity party. After forcing myself through my normal morning routine in what seemed slow motion, I stuffed my "To Do" list in my purse and hit the road, trying to ignore my physical discomfort.

Pulling into a local grocery store parking lot later that day, I heaved a sigh as I checked off the last item on my errand list. *Soon*, I thought, *I'll be homeward bound*. Physically drained and overstressed, I dragged myself into the store in spite of the temptation to skip this last stop.

After a non-eventful trip through the produce department, I headed to my car and flung a bag of oranges into the back seat. After swinging the door shut, a middle-aged woman seemed to appear from nowhere. Distraught and crying uncontrollably, she pointed to the newspaper in her trembling hands. "My son..." she cried, "he was murdered." Seeing a photo of her and her son, I read the headline: "Mother Marks Day of Slain Son's Birth."

I wrapped my arms around the stranger and held her for what seemed an eternity. I wept. She cried more. In a heavenly moment, God enabled me to share this mourning mother's burden.

Maria's son, Peter, had been beaten to death during a drug-related robbery five months earlier. The next day would be the anniversary of his birth, and as written in the news story, she had planned a party at a local park to celebrate Peter's life.

As a mom of three, I couldn't begin to fathom losing a child, especially under such horrific circumstances. "I can't imagine how painful it must be to have lost your son," I told

Maria, "but there's One who does know, and He can bring the comfort and peace you need."

Before we parted ways, I asked Maria if I could pray for her. There, among abandoned grocery carts and curious bystanders, we joined hands and together brought the burden of her son's death to Jesus. We both left with a lighter load.

On the way home, I cried for Maria's loss, but thanked God for sending her to me. Others, misunderstanding her fragile emotional state, might have rejected her in her time of need. Because God knew that I would embrace Maria, He orchestrated the perfect timing for us to be in the right place at the right time.

The next day I attended Peter's birthday celebration where I stayed in the sidelines observing the emotionally charged scene. As people from across the city released a rainbow of balloons into the sky, Maria and my eyes met when she hugged a loved one. Peeking over her friend's shoulder, she smiled through her tears and gave a little wave. Words weren't necessary.

It's easy to become so overwhelmed and caught up in our own whirlwind of trials that we don't recognize other people's needs. God wants to use us to help others, even while we're in our greatest time of need—*if we're available.*

God designed wilderness seasons with divine appointments that you won't want to miss. Even when your suffering is at its climax, He divinely orchestrates opportunities for you to sow into others' lives. And as you refresh others, you yourself will be refreshed! (See Proverbs 11:25.)

God may call on you day or night, often giving no advance notice of what lies ahead. Whatever the timing, He prepared you in advance for the assignment! (See Ephesians 2:10.)

Make yourself available for God's use in the wilderness. If He can use a worn-out, burnt-out, and stressed-out mom to deliver a Heaven-sent hug, He can use you—if you're available.

Being available to God isn't as complicated as we often make it. In some ways it can be likened to the "Simon Says" game often played at childhood birthday parties. When the leader commanded, "Simon says...Put your hands in the air," those following Simon's directions shot their hands in the air. But if the leader said, "Put your hands in the air," those raising their hands were quickly disqualified from the game because they acted without hearing "Simon says."

I never progressed very far in that game, because instead of listening to and responding only to what "Simon said," my knee jerk reactions led me to follow misguided directions before Simon gave the command.

Imagine what we could accomplish for God if we not only made ourselves available to Him, but also listened and responded only to His direction and command. Imagine the wood, hay, and stubble that would go up in smoke!

The Bible says that Jesus, our perfect example, did only as His Father commanded Him (see John 14:31). Jesus didn't act on need, pressure from society, intimidation, expectation, or because He wanted to win a popularity contest.

He listened to and responded only to His Father's direction, even walking past some who could have benefited greatly by His divine gifting.

When God healed the crippled beggar at the gate Beautiful through the hands of Peter and John, it caused quite a stir (see Acts 3). Learning that the name of Jesus healed the crippled man, leaders seized Peter and John and warned them not to teach in the name of Jesus. They wanted to silence these bold apostles—just as the enemy wants to silence you!

But Peter and John knew they must obey God, who had commanded them to preach the Gospel. Instead of obeying man, they obeyed God, asking Him to enable them to speak with even greater boldness—and to confirm His word with miraculous signs and wonders. And God did! (See Acts 4:29-31 and 5:12.)

Being brought on the carpet again, the high priest reminded Peter and John of the warning *not* to preach Jesus. But they replied: *"We must obey God rather than men!"* (Acts 5:29) Their response got them a severe flogging. Following God and not people often comes with a price.

Being unmoved by people's criticism—or people's praise—won't win us any popularity contests. But avoiding being swayed by people's opinions will position us to do the work of Jesus: the Father's will.

Countless needs and people cry for our attention in the wilderness and in the Promised Land alike. But if we follow Jesus as our role model, we will refuse to cave in to the pressures of people—even if some don't understand or are disappointed. As Peter and John said, "It is better to obey God than man."

Well-meaning people, especially experienced wilderness travelers, sometimes offer direction to those walking through wilderness seasons. Spiritual counsel or advice aren't always words of wisdom and, therefore, can harm us instead of benefitting us. Misguided, though well-intended, words of wisdom can send us on the wrong course and increase the suffering from which we're trying to get free!

Take time to seek the Father, and ask Him what your next move ought to be. If Father says, "Do it!" then do it; and if Father says, "Don't do it!" then don't do it. But if Father isn't directing the moves, stay put until He reveals the next play.

Just as God connected me with Maria at just the right moment, God supernaturally and purposefully connects us with chosen people as if throwing desert life preservers.

The way in which God connects people reminds me of one of my favorite childhood memories: dot-to-dot activity books. I used to sit for hours connecting the numbered dots, watching pictures of all sorts develop before my eyes. With mounting anticipation of what my dot-to-dot might create, I often raced through the numbers with lightning speed.

As part of His ultimate plan, God ordained certain individuals as DOTS in our lives. Along our earthly journey—and on our wilderness sojourn—God orchestrates divine appointments to join us with those He designed to complete our life's picture. Connecting one DOT at a time—in His perfect time—God reveals the heavenly work of art He envisioned for our life.

You might be surprised when some DOTS appear in your life picture, as they often arrive unannounced and with little fanfare. DOTS are critical in the wilderness experience, and missing even one connection will not only leave the picture incomplete, it can prolong the wilderness season!

On the first day of Bible school, a stunning woman whose eyes shined with the light of the Holy Spirit plopped her suitcase by my cot and randomly chose the bed next to mine. A DOT had arrived!

Between classes and studies, an ocean of tears flowed as Becky and I laughed and cried over life issues. Not only did Becky become a lifelong personal friend, but God continues to deepen our relationship, blessing us with keys to propel us forward in God's Kingdom plan. I love this DOT!

Becky, a gift God used to encourage me in the wilderness, made herself available when I needed to vent and never judged me in my weaknesses. Although she allowed me to express my discouragement and weariness, she always pointed me to God's plan and promises. She saw beyond my suffering and believed in the fulfillment of God's purpose for my life and ministry. Becky wouldn't let me quit, reminding me regularly about God's faithfulness. She was always available for prayer and often called with a timely word of encouragement that dripped like honey into my soul.

Another DOT awaited me at a women's luncheon where I was scheduled to speak. Prior to delivering my message, the group enjoyed a luscious meal and tender time of fellowship. When Carol's and my eyes met from across the long table, my heart pinged. Another DOT had arrived!

Carol and I soon discovered our shared passion for women's ministry and to this day continue to seek God's plan to touch women with the hope and healing Jesus offers. I love this DOT too!

Early on my wilderness journey, I had accepted Carol's invitation to be the keynote speaker at her women's conference in St. John, Washington. I didn't realize the increased challenges I would face as the conference neared.

Carol, knowing the circumstances of my suffering, would have graciously allowed me to cancel my speaking engagement commitment, though she never suggested it. I suspect that she considered offering me the option of canceling, willing to find someone else to fill my spot, but she didn't even broach the subject.

If Carol would have provided a way out, I would likely have taken it, as the thought of developing, preparing, and delivering the messages for the conference overwhelmed me and seemed impossible. With God's help, the conference was a huge success, and although I felt physically weak, God was strong and enabled me to minister a message that brought healing and hope to the women.

Throughout my wilderness journey, Carol sent letters of encouragement and peanut M&Ms, e-mailed regularly, and with steadfast faith in the unchanging Word of God, kept

His promises before me. Carol, like Becky, wouldn't let me quit.

When a pastor encouraged the congregation to greet one another during a church service, I met another treasured DOT. "I'm Marcia," she said after I introduced myself, "and this is my soon to be ex-husband Doug."

Was she serious? I wondered as the service continued.

She was. Although divorce proceedings had been set in motion and a firm court date had been scheduled, God intervened and healed their marriage. In the process, He granted me a lifelong friendship with this couple, who reached countless times into my wilderness with loving kindness and selfless sacrifice.

While I battled health issues on several fronts, Marcia stepped in, flying to Spokane to fill in as a mother and standing by me as a friend. In spite of her demanding career as an engineer, she showed up to help after surgeries or to entertain the kids while I recovered from medical procedures. Marcia, bringing laughter to our family, eased pain and lightened heavy hearts.

I regularly ask God to reveal my DOTS—those with which He chooses to connect me in fulfilling His divine will. I ask Him to firmly establish my DOT relationships, sending the roots in Christ deep where they cannot be shaken by life's storms.

Allow God to bring DOT relationships to your life that drive you toward Him and His purpose—and ask Him to enable you to let go of other relationships that might unknowingly woo you away from God. The Lord honors this petition and will connect—and disconnect—the DOTS in the most loving ways.

If you happen to find yourself doing a dot-to-dot—or eating a box of DOTS—may it remind you to ask God to reveal His chosen DOTS. He will connect you, one DOT at a time, until His perfect masterpiece is complete.

For Reflection and Discussion

1. In what ways have you made yourself available to your Father? Have you been available to help others as you've journeyed in the wilderness or have you been too focused on your suffering to notice other people's needs?

2. Reflect on the activities in which you're currently involved. Examine your motives for each activity. Did you seek your Father's direction? Do you have pruning to do in your life so you can be more fruitful or are you on course? Explain.

3. Think about your DOTS, those who have impacted you the most when you needed it the most. Write each one a note of thanks and tell them how they have influenced you.

4. How much does people's criticism influence what you do and how you feel? How much does people's praise influence what you do and how you feel?

Reflect on what I am saying, for the Lord will give you insight into all this (2 Timothy 2:7).

Prayer of Repentance

Lord God, I've been so selfish and preoccupied with my suffering. I sometimes feel I must wait until my life is in order before You can use me, and sometimes forget that You want to use me right where I am. I humble myself before You and ask that You would use my life to bring You glory, even as I continue my journey in the wilderness. I'm sorry for the times I've missed opportunities to share Your love with others. Forgive me too, gracious Father, for establishing plans for my life based on the pressure, criticism, and praise of man instead of surrendering to You and following Your direction.

Other areas of repentance:

Repent, then, and turn to God, so that your sins may be wiped out, that times of refreshing may come from the Lord (Acts 3:19).

Prayer of Submission

Amazing Lord of my life, thank You for exposing areas of my life that need to change so I can be more like You. I give You my life, Father, though I feel weak and incapable. Use me, even in my weakness, to demonstrate Your love and grace. Grant me increased discernment as I cross paths with others in need. Enable me to speak words of encouragement when I am discouraged, to smile when I feel like frowning, and to listen when someone needs a caring friend. Fill me daily, Lord of life, so I can pour into those You bring across my path. In Jesus' name.

Other areas of submission:

Submit yourselves, then, to God (James 4:7).

My Personal Words From My Father

_____

_____

_____

Speak, Lord, for Your servant is listening (1 Samuel 3:9).

From the Father's Heart

My chosen vessel, I have poured out My love into your heart by My Holy Spirit. When you are weak, I am strong. When you are unable, I will enable you. When you are ill-equipped, I will equip you. For the lives I shall touch through your weakness is an important work and has been ordained by Me since the beginning. Every life is important to Me. Every detail matters to Me. As you make yourself available to Me, and surrender your plan to My plan, I will use you when you least expect it.

Chapter 14

Expecting

Meditation

Though I wait with joyful expectation, I must know that my Father heard my plea, and must trust His perfect timing and wondrous ways of bringing the answers I need.

Scripture Focus:

In the morning, O Lord, You hear my voice; in the morning I lay my requests before You and wait in expectation (Psalm 5:3).

What is my Father speaking to me through this Scripture?

May my meditation be pleasing to Him, as I rejoice in the Lord (Psalm 104:34).

God's Perfect Timing

In September 2006, faith rose when I remembered the prophetic word I had received in 2003: "Your breakthrough is coming at 46." My 46th birthday would arrive on October 28, 2006, only a month away!

I had it all figured out. Since my anticipated breakthrough would come at 46, I determined that it should arrive the *first* day of my 46th year. It made perfect sense!

My faith skyrocketed when a notice arrived in the mail: FIRST NATIONAL DAY OF HEALING—OCTOBER 28, 2006. Charles and Francis Hunter were spearheading the first national day of healing on my 46th birthday—my planned day of breakthrough! People across the globe were praying and fasting, expecting a tidal wave of healing that would go down in history. Healing Rooms across the country would open doors on October 28th so people could receive prayer and healing.

Preparing to catch the anticipated wave of divine healing, I started a 21-day Daniel fast, more than ready for my breakthrough after a long five years in the wilderness. On October 16, I wrote in my journal:

> I've been walking through the most difficult season of my life. Since I began documenting and proclaiming God's miracles, I've come under tremendous attack. I've seen countless doctors, endured endless tests, taken truckloads of medications, endured numerous surgeries, procedures and other misery, but to no avail. I'm weak, suffer debilitating fatigue, every bone and joint aches, my arms are numb, my fingers tingle, I have tremors, trouble walking and swallowing, mysterious lumps appear, I can't sleep, complications from surgeries plague me and new maladies continue to crop up. I wonder if I'm dying.

October 28th came and went with no miracle birthday present. Yet because of the inner work God had done in me as I walked through the wilderness, I wasn't disappointed nor did I even entertain the thought that my unworthiness had caused God to deny my healing. Instead of stashing another disappointment in the secret chamber of my heart—as that chamber no longer existed—I pressed on, doing what I knew to do, loving and trusting God with all my heart to the best of my ability.

I continued to stand on God's Word for my healing provision, but trusted God's timing and ways. I knew He loved me, so if my continued suffering was acceptable to Him, it was acceptable to me. Although more than ready for breakthrough, I had entered a beautiful place of rest that was not dependent on my circumstances.

Though God had done and continued a deep work of restoration in my life, days of discouragement still visited occasionally like an uninvited guest. One particularly difficult day, I was again feeling sorry for myself because I had waited so long for God to come through for me.

While preparing a special family dinner, I thought of how I had waited—and waited—for my miracle and expected it to come as I had ordered. I had prayed the right prayers, confessed the right Scriptures, and had received anointed ministry from the right ministries. Yet I was still sick! Expressing tear-filled disappointment, I told God that the answer He was sending was *not* the answer for which I was looking.

When I opened the cupboard in search of basil, a neatly aligned spice rack greeted me. All bottles were lined up like soldiers, identical except for their contents. Scanning multiple rows of spices and seasonings, I found no basil. Certain I had the common seasoning, I touched each bottle's identification label with my fingertip, searching and researching each row.

Cinnamon...thyme...oregano...cumin...cloves...tarragon...allspice...salt...but no basil. As a last effort, I rummaged through a cupboard of overflow seasonings. None.

Spotting a half-hidden bottle with no identification label, I thought, *Well? It's green. It'll have to do for now.* Because of a pre-dinner time crunch, I couldn't afford a last-minute trip to the grocery store. I sprinkled the mystery seasoning over the chicken, asking God to bless the meal in spite of my questionable adjustment.

Opening the same cupboard to reach for the salt, I froze. There, in front, stood a large bottle marked BASIL. Staring in disbelief, I could almost hear it announce, "Here I am!"

How could I have possibly missed that! I wondered. Three times the size of the other bottles, the basil made its presence known. But because I had expected a small bottle that matched the others, I missed out on the very thing that would have met my need.

Imagine what Elijah might have expected when the Lord said, *"Go out and stand on the mountain in the presence of the Lord, for the Lord is about to pass by"* (1 Kings 19:11). No doubt Elijah was on the lookout for an obvious sign!

First, a great and powerful wind tore the mountains apart and shattered the rocks, but the Lord was not in the wind. Next an earthquake came, then fire, but the Lord wasn't in the earthquake or the fire. Instead of showing Himself in the obvious, God revealed Himself with a soft whisper.

God's presence came in a way Elijah likely didn't expect. Yet, if he had not been spiritually in tune, he might have missed God's gentle whisper, like I missed the basil!

Reflecting on the disappointment I had expressed earlier regarding God's answer (or lack of an answer) to my prayer for deliverance, I realized I had been looking only for the answer I wanted. But God, in His sovereignty and love, was sending His reply in a package I didn't recognize.

Knowing God is a faithful, loving Father who always knows best, I smiled and once again whispered, "Have Your way, Lord." Discouragement fled, and I knew I could wait— forever if I had to.

For Reflection and Discussion

1. In what ways have you tried to plan your escape from the wilderness? Explain.

2. When your suffering is prolonged, or intensified, how do you respond to God? How do you respond to others?

3. Reflect on the words you speak during extended trials. Do your words align with the promises of God's Word or do your words indicate that you've given up?

Make note of three Scriptures you are standing on as you wait on God. Speak them daily.

4. Talk to your Father about what you're feeling at this point of your wilderness journey. Your Father knows what you're feeling even before you express it and He invites you to pour out your heart, including anger, frustration, weariness.

Reflect on what I am saying, for the Lord will give you insight into all this (2 Timothy 2:7).

Prayer of Repentance

I thought I had it all figured out, Father. I expected You to do things My way and hoped You'd bring an end to my suffering when and how I felt best. I'm sorry, loving Father, for thinking I had the answers, when I really know so little, if anything. I wanted You to answer my needs a certain way, instead of trusting You to bring everything to pass in the way You choose to do so. I offer You my stained garment of sin, and ask You, again, to wash me clean.

Other areas of repentance:

Repent, then, and turn to God, so that your sins may be wiped out, that times of refreshing may come from the Lord (Acts 3:19).

Prayer of Submission

Here I am again, Father, coming before You in submission wearing a garment of praise and thanks. How quickly I stumble and try to go my own way, but how quickly You help me back on the right path. I surrender my ways to You once again, and ask that You have Your way in me. Though my suffering continues, I want You to accomplish everything in me that You intend to accomplish in this season. Your timing and Your ways are acceptable to me, Father God. Let me learn all I can learn in this place, that I might teach others in coming days. In Jesus' name.

Other areas of submission:

Submit yourselves, then, to God (James 4:7).

My Personal Words From My Father

Speak, Lord, for Your servant is listening (1 Samuel 3:9).

From the Father's Heart

My child, I cherish you. I delight in seeing you grow. Much of what I am doing in you now, you are not even aware of. For it is an inner work, a deep work of the heart that no man can see with the human eye. My glory rests on you, even in the state that you are in, and My favor surrounds you, even in the place you feel uneasy. Though you have pondered the ways in which your season of wilderness shall come to an end, My master plan shall prevail. It is not your deliverance, but the wilderness, that is producing fruitfulness in you that others will partake of for generations to come.

Chapter 15

Suddenly

Meditation

My Father is a God of suddenlies!

Scripture Focus

About midnight Paul and Silas were praying and singing hymns to God, and the other prisoners were listening to them. Suddenly there was such a violent earthquake that the foundations of the prison were shaken. At once all the prison doors flew open, and everybody's chains came loose (Acts 16:25-26).

What is my Father speaking to me through this Scripture?

May my meditation be pleasing to Him, as I rejoice in the Lord (Psalm 104:34).

Fulfillment of Prophetic Promise

On April 11, 2007, my most recent book, *Extraordinary Miracles in the Lives of Ordinary People*, was released. After the mail carrier handed me the package from my publisher,

I closed the door, tore open the package, and stared at the cover. Overcome with emotion, I sensed the sudden fluttering in my stomach.

Flooded with emotion, tears dripped on the entryway tile floor. "How did You do this, God?" I cried. "How did You do this?...through *me?*"

Although physically drained after a long and difficult wilderness birth, seeing the fruit of that labor energized me. This book of God's wondrous miracles was itself a miracle.

With great joy I had listened to extraordinary testimonies of God's work in the earth, rejoicing with each one who had received a special miracle. Each unique story had strengthened my faith for the breakthrough for which I was still waiting.

The day after the book arrived, I awoke feeling as if two ice picks had been lodged in my eyeballs and two more in the base of my skull. I was scheduled to attend A Company of Women ministry meeting at Stormy and Rosalie Storment's home in Post Falls, Idaho, that evening, where I planned to spend the night.

Although I debated with myself about canceling as I hadn't found any relief from the migraine, I headed to Post Falls in spite of my hesitation.

Pulling off the freeway just over the Idaho/Washington border, I contemplated returning home. The pain medication I had taken earlier had made me nauseous and my head was throbbing from squinting in the sunlight. Although going home seemed like a reasonable option, I pulled back onto the freeway and continued my journey.

Immediately before the meeting began, Cynthia Steele and her team from Solid Rock Christian Center arrived. Although everyone else seemed to know this godly woman, I had never met nor heard of her, or the women accompanying her. These beautiful women wore humility like a garment, obviously there to serve, not to be served.

After Cynthia preached a powerful message from God's Word, her ministry team joined her to pray for women. Jacqueline Johnson, one of the prophetic team, pointed at me, then motioned for me to come forward first. "The Lord told me to pray for your healing," she said.

Prayer for healing was not new to me. Over the past several years I had received healing prayer from numerous people and ministries, had visited the Healing Rooms, and spoken the promises from God's Word over my body on a regular basis. Yet tonight, God had pointed me out to Jacqueline and directed her to pray for me.

"Lift your hands in the receiving position," Jacque said. Then, with a booming authority like I had never heard before, Jacque prayed:

Father, I thank You that You have taken this precious vessel into the next level of healing that You have for her. Father, I speak to every system in her body now and I command it to line up and function even as it was supposed to function before the fall of man. I command everything in her body to come into proper alignment now in the name of Jesus. I speak to every organ, every tissue, every muscle, every bone, and every joint in her and I command and call everything into normalcy within her body from the crown of her head to the soles of her feet. The death threat that the enemy has out, we cancel the assignment now in the name of Jesus. Every word he has brought to her of untimely death, we cancel it now in the name of Jesus and we apply the blood of Jesus to every area and aspect of her being. Spirit of fear, where you have arisen and tried to have dominion, we break your power and the authority of it now in the name of Jesus. We pronounce the Word of God over her that the perfect love of God will cast out every hint of fear. Everything that has tried to come as a detriment to circumvent the plan and vision God has for her life, we command death and destruction to it now in the name of Jesus. We cast down every imagination and every high thing that exalts itself against the knowledge of God in her life now in the name of Jesus. We decree and declare now that He who has begun a good work in her will bring it to completion, to the day of Jesus Christ. We thank You for the report of the doctor because now we know what to do with it. Father, as she stands before You tonight, facing any fear she may have had, reports she has heard, and any words that have lodged in her spirit, she will rise up in the authority that You have given her and will walk in her healing. We pronounce divine health over her from the crown of her head to the soles of her feet. And Father, may she be surrounded with people who are going to speak Your Word and Your desire for her into her life and into her spirit. We bless You and honor You for it, in Jesus' name.

Next Adalina Carter stepped forward, placed her hand on my shoulder, and prayed:

I take authority in the name of Jesus against every curse that has been spoken to you, to your mother, to all the women and generations in your family. I command that those words fall to the ground and produce no fruit in the name of Jesus. I call forth every blessing that has been spoken over you, your mother, and all the women in your family. And from this moment on you will walk in the blessing and not the curses, in the name of Jesus.

Prophetess Cynthia Steele then lifted her hand and prayed:

The Lord says that you have sensed in your spirit that there is a high calling in your life, but it seems like the calling that you're sensing and where you are seems like eons away from each other. But God says I am taking you through the process of development and training and I am building you. God says I am establishing you and building you. The Lord says don't be weary with those processes because I am the one who gave the call and I will see to it that the fulfillment comes to pass. And God shows me that He has you on a runway and you've been running and running, but there's also been some weariness because the level of your expectation and where you're running have not matched up. But God says He doesn't want you to be weary. He says your fight and your labor hasn't been in vain. God wants to speak into your spirit tonight that you would run on with that baton and run high because God says there's a high calling on you and God says I'm taking you into high places. And the Lord says that even though things came to slow you up and to hinder you or tie up your feet, He says don't pay attention to those things but keep your eye on the prize. He says if you keep your eye on the prize that you're going to run and you're going to receive that prize. I sense the Lord wants to tell you that there's greatness down on the inside of you. You're going some places in God. I don't care what the enemy has thrown your way to block you. It's almost like he's trying to cut you off at the pass before you ever get out of the gate. You sense this overwhelming great depth of something God wants to do with you in your spirit man. Your spirit man has already embraced the destiny that's down on the inside of you. But I see that there have been so many things that have tried to come to hinder you, block you, and discourage you from the greatness that you feel in here. But God says, I'm going to bring it to pass. You don't have to worry about that. I'm going to complete and fulfill everything that I've spoken over you and everything that I said I would do. You're going to see the fulfillment of it. In fact God says, when I get done walking you through these processes, you're going to teach My Word and you're going to teach and train women how to walk in realms of excellence and glory because God says you would have already walked through it because I'm taking you through the school of learning. You're going to know those precious indentations and those places and depths and clefts in the rock. God says I'm going to teach them to you and as I teach those things to you, then you're going to turn around and teach those things to others. God says you're going to be a prolific teacher. I see you standing and teaching and preaching the Word of God with fire and the anointing under the unction of the Holy Ghost. So know that the greatness that you're feeling in your spiritual womb, He is going to bring it to full development and completion. God says hold on to that word; speak it over yourself. I see discouragement coming at different seasons in your life in times past, almost like a wet cloth trying to put out the fire, but every time there's something in you that's a fighter and you stand up and fight; and it'll come again and you'll rise up and fight. God's building something precious and powerful down on the inside of you and it's going to be dynamic in its operation. So you be encouraged! Amen.

When I returned to my seat, Faye Higbee, a precious pastor friend handed me a note that read:

You are worthy by the righteous blood of the lamb. You are a golden princess of the Most High God and that is the platform from which you will operate from this day forward. Healed, blessed, chosen. Love, Jesus.

Shortly after the meeting ended, I stuffed the note in my Bible and excused myself for bed as my head was still throbbing. Although I'd like to say that my faith was soaring, I drifted off to sleep with no spiritual expectations whatsoever.

Thinking it was morning, I awoke with my eyes squeezed shut, trying to avoid the blazing light shining in my face. Because many large windows graced the room where I slept, I suspected I had forgotten to close the blinds before climbing under the covers the night before. But when I opened my eyes, the room was pitch black. All blinds were shut. Seeing 3:00 A.M. on the digital clock, I realized it was still the middle of the night. I drifted back to sleep, not thinking anything of it.

Waking up as I did any other morning, I braced for the pain and stiffness I normally experienced. But something was different! Like a flapjack, I flipped from one side to the other. No pain! *No* discomfort anywhere in my body.

I didn't have to wake up my arms as the numbness and tingling were gone. My bones and joints didn't ache. The hand and head tremors were nowhere to be found. My temples weren't pounding.

Sitting on the side of the bed, I raised my arms above my head. I hadn't been able to do that for years! Because my arms often felt like lead weights, I could only lift them slightly and briefly, limiting my full expression of praise.

I leapt out of bed, making a beeline for my suitcase. I lifted it effortlessly—again—and again—and again—and again. The fibro fogginess had vanished; my mind was crystal clear, and I was full of energy.

When I had least expected it—after 226 doctor appointments and procedures, 4 surgeries, 1915 painkillers, and 163 prescriptions, my breakthrough had arrived. And it came at 46—just as God had prophesied through Mary Jenkins in 2003!

Although seeing a long list of physical maladies disappear overnight was a marvelous medical miracle, it paled in comparison to the transformation God did in my heart *while I waited for my breakthrough* in the wilderness.

I remembered the dream, seeing the speaker who appeared to have been clothed in God's glory, radiating unspeakable joy as she proclaimed, "My Father loves me! He *LOVES* me!" But now, no longer an audience spectator longing to know the Father's love, I *knew* the Father's love.

My Father loved me! *Through the wilderness, I found what I had searched for all my life!* The revelation of God's love, hidden treasure discovered in the darkness of trial, brought a glorious transformation that changed me forever. Knowing that God loves me—not because of what I can do for Him—enabled me to break out of the cocoon of suffering, prepared to fly.

In the midst of the seeming waste and suffering of the wilderness lay God's hidden purposes. I hadn't done everything right; I hadn't prayed enough or read the Bible enough; I hadn't done enough for God and hadn't sensed His presence—yet God's grace granted me a revelation of His love. And His grace will do it for you too!

Song of Solomon says in 8:5, *"Who is this coming up from the wilderness, leaning upon her beloved?"* (NKJV) Having learned to love and trust my Beloved, I emerged from the wilderness no longer leaning on the arm of the flesh, but instead leaning on my beloved Father God, who loves me—and you!

Weariness and discouragement can tempt wilderness travelers to quit, especially if they're suffering through a long-term wilderness season. When the season lingers as it did for me, it can seem like God doesn't care or has forgotten that we even exist.

If we're battle-weary, hopelessness can take root and tempt us to lay down the God-given dreams and promises that led us to pursue the Promised Land in the first place. "Yup," the enemy suggests, launching missiles of negative thoughts. "The promise you *thought* God made to you just wasn't the plan for you...you didn't qualify for the prize... you must have missed God on that one...you may as well just let it go. You've waited so long and it's obviously not going to happen." And the list goes on.

Coming into agreement with the enemy's lies empowers him to drag us further down the slippery slope of hopelessness. Then we risk not only laying down God's dreams and promises, but letting them die. "Yup," the enemy's voice rises again, "surely God didn't give you that dream. He didn't make that promise. Let it die. There's no life there anyway! It's dead. May as well just bury it because there's *no* hope."

If something dies, it *is* hopeless—that is, until Jesus arrives on the scene!

When Jesus received word that Lazarus was sick He said, *"This sickness will not end in death. No, it is for God's glory so that God's Son may be glorified through it"* (John 11:4).

The Bible says that Jesus loved Lazarus and his sisters Mary and Martha (see John 11:5). Yet after hearing that Lazarus was sick, He waited two more days before even heading in their direction! One might believe it odd for someone claiming to love His friends to be so slow to respond to their dire need.

By the time Jesus arrived, Lazarus had been in the tomb for four days. Martha, and later Mary, said, *"Lord, if You had been here, my brother would not have died"* (John 11:21,32). These sisters were operating on their time schedule. But Jesus was operating on Heaven's time schedule—and Heaven is *never* late.

"Where have you laid him?" Jesus asked. Coming to the tomb where a stone was laid across the entrance, Jesus said, "Take away the stone."

Martha warned that because her brother had been in the tomb for four days, there would be a bad odor, yet Jesus asked them to remove the stone. Jesus said, "Did I not tell you that if you believed, *you would see the glory of God?*"

After they took away the stone, Jesus thanked His Father, then called, "Lazarus, come out!" Lazarus, who had *no hope, no life*, and *no future*, arose from the dead!

The wilderness season you're walking through will *not* end in death to the dreams God has given you. The wilderness season you're walking through will *not* end in death to the promises God made to you. NO! The wilderness season you're walking through *is for God's glory so that God's Son may be glorified **through** it.*

It might seem like Jesus has taken too long to come. You, like Mary, may have even said, "Lord, if You had been here, my dream wouldn't have died."

Where have you laid the dreams God gave you? Where have you laid the promises He made to you? Take Jesus to the tomb where you buried those dreams and promises.

But Lord, you might be thinking, *they've been dead for a long time. It might stink!* As Jesus said to Martha, He says to you: "Did I not tell you that if you believe, you will see the glory of God?"

The God-given promises and dreams that you thought were dead and buried—*are not dead.* The promises and dreams that the devil has tried to convince you were dead and buried—*are not dead.* They may be sleeping, but they're *not dead. Every* dream God deposited in you will surely come to pass, and *every* promise God made to you will surely be fulfilled.

Jesus is alive today and He's at the tomb of your heart. The same resurrection power that raised Lazarus—and Jesus—from the dead is available to you today. "Take away the stone," Jesus says. Push aside the stone from the dead and buried dreams and promises, call them forth today, in the name of Jesus, and watch them arise to fulfill their full life expectancy.

Your heavenly Father, who loves you, will make a way for you when there seems to be no way. God has a plan for you—*a good plan!*

In the desert prepare the way for the Lord; make straight in the wilderness a highway for our God. Every valley shall be raised up, every mountain and hill made low; the rough ground shall become level, the rugged places a plain. And the glory of the Lord will be revealed, and all mankind together will see it. For the mouth of the Lord has spoken (Isaiah 40:3-5).

Today's wilderness is tomorrow's testimony. Don't quit! It will be well worth the wait!

For Reflection and Discussion

1. Your Father's hidden purposes often lie in the seeming waste and suffering. What hidden treasures have you discovered through your suffering?

2. Did you take Jesus to the tomb where you buried the dreams or promises He gave you? Did you allow your Father to breathe resurrection life into those dreams and promises?

3. What have you learned about your Father while traveling through the pages of this wilderness journey? Looking back to the dream shared in Chapter 1, do you now relate more to the one in the audience, longing for the Father's love, or to the speaker, who is delighted in knowing the Father's love? Explain.

4. Say, "I am worthy by the righteous blood of the Lamb. I am a golden prince/princess of the Most High God and that is the platform from which I will operate from this day forward. Healed, blessed, chosen. My Father loves me!"

Reflect on what I am saying, for the Lord will give you insight into all this (2 Timothy 2:7).

Prayer of Repentance

Father God, I need Your grace to forgive me for doubting Your love, for questioning Your faithfulness, and for second-guessing Your plan for my life. Instead of standing on Your truth, I believed the lies of the enemy. You blessed me with Your promises, You've given me dreams, yet I became weary and wanted to give up. I have no excuse for the error of my ways, but come before Your throne of grace to find Your mercy. I have fallen short in so many ways, O Lord. I'm sorry, Father, for resisting the love You've so graciously bestowed upon me. I need Your love, O God. And I need You. In Jesus' name.

Other areas of repentance:

Repent, then, and turn to God, so that your sins may be wiped out, that times of refreshing may come from the Lord (Acts 3:19).

Prayer of Submission

Dear Father God of power and might, You brought me from the wilderness to the miraculous, leading me on a wondrous journey to Your love. God of wonders, You breathed resurrection life into that which I allowed to die. I rejoice in You and thank You! Though I thought I had missed the mark and had failed, You arrived right on time to give me new hope. I commit, Father, to serve You all the days of my life and submit myself to You, body, soul, and spirit. And as we go forth, I shall lean on You, my Beloved Father. In Jesus' name.

Other areas of submission:

Submit yourselves, then, to God (James 4:7).

My Personal Words From My Father

Speak, Lord, for Your servant is listening (1 Samuel 3:9).

From the Father's Heart

Though you have waited with expectation for Me, I have waited with expectation for you! Remember, My child, that I laid out all the days of your life before a single day passed. Nothing you face in coming days will be unexpected to Me. I know what is coming and have a perfect plan for every day of your life. Follow Me, trust Me, and receive My love. I love it when you love Me. Go now, into all the world and show them My love. I will never leave you nor forsake you. We will walk together forever.

About Therese Marszalek

Spokane author and columnist Therese Marszalek is a dynamic speaker and freelance writer. Her monthly column appeared in the *Inland NW Christian News* from 2000 until its final issue in 2008, and over 350 of her articles have appeared in multi-denominational publications across the country. An ordained minister and founder of Breaking Out Ministries, Therese has a M.A. Div and she completed Rhema Bible School.

Her books include *Extraordinary Miracles in the Lives of Ordinary People* (also released in audio), *Miracles Still Happen*, *Breaking Out*, and *Take Her off the Pedestal: She's Just Like You*, a book to encourage and inspire women, is pending publication.

Therese has enjoyed numerous radio and television interviews. She appeared in *Miracles in Our Midst (and Heroes Among Us: Miracles Around Us)*, a Grizzly Adams production that highlighted her book *Miracles Still Happen*, which has aired on several networks including TBN (also in DVD). She was a guest on *The Testimony of Jesus* television program reaching 66 million and appeared on the Morris Cerullo

Helpline television program, filmed before a live audience at the CBS studios in Hollywood, reaching over 2.4 billion people in 140 nations.

Therese is passionate about bringing people hope and healing through Jesus Christ and His Word. She has spoken at numerous conferences and events; her messages challenge people to walk closer to Christ and bring encouragement to the weary. Known for her transparency and spiritual depth, Therese draws her audience to a place of vulnerability where God can do His greatest work of transformation.

Active in women's ministries since being born again in 1979, Therese's genuine love for God and people breathes hope into the hopeless. Her personal experience of searching for Christian truth and longing for a more intimate relationship with Christ birthed her speaking and writing ministry as well as her contagious zeal for discipleship in the Body of Christ. She also has developed and taught Christian writers' seminars with great success.

Therese lives in Spokane, Washington, with her husband and two of their children. Their son is serving in the U.S. Army. Her step children, who hold a special place in Therese's heart, live in the Seattle area.

You may contact Therese at:

> **Web site:**
> **www.breakingoutministries.com.**

Other Books By Therese Marszalek

Extraordinary Miracles in the Lives of Ordinary People
(Harrison House)

Miracles Still Happen (Harrison House)

Breaking Out (Publish America)